POLICE MANAGEMENT FOR THE 1990s
A Practitioner's Road Map

ABOUT THE AUTHOR

John Bizzack is a Captain with the Lexington, Kentucky, Division of Police where he serves as a commander in the Criminal Investigation Section. A graduate from Eastern Kentucky University, he has served in Patrol and Traffic assignments prior to holding various investigative and detective supervisory positions for the past twelve years. He holds degrees in Criminal Justice and Business Management.

He has authored published articles appearing in criminal justice periodicals and is the recipient of nearly two-hundred letters of recognition and achievement, awards and commendations from his own department, from other law enforcement agencies, and from the private business sector. These recognitions have been given for his work in various phases of law enforcement, investigations, administration, management, and community involvement.

Captain Bizzack is an instructor, certified through the Kentucky Law Enforcement Council. He has and is serving on various state and local boards and task forces dealing with contemporary issues facing police service and other components of the criminal justice system.

POLICE MANAGEMENT
FOR THE 1990s
A Practitioner's Road Map

By

JOHN BIZZACK

Captain
Criminal Investigation Section
Division of Police
Lexington, Kentucky

CHARLES C THOMAS • PUBLISHER
Springfield • Illinois • U.S.A.

Published and Distributed Throughout the World by

CHARLES C THOMAS • PUBLISHER
2600 South First Street
Springfield, Illinois 62794-9265

© *1989 by* CHARLES C THOMAS • PUBLISHER

ISBN 0-398-05583-1

Library of Congress Catalog Card Number: 89-4368

Printed in the United States of America
SC-R-3

Library of Congress Cataloging-in-Publication Data

Bizzack, John.
    Police management for the 1990s : a practitioner's road map / John
Bizzack.
       p.   cm.
    Bibliography: p.
    Includes index.
    ISBN 0-398-05583-1
    1. Police administration—United States.   I. Title.
HV8141.B59   1989
350.74'0973—dc 19

                89-4368
                CIP

This book is dedicated to the one person who, more than anyone else, has influenced and taught me the excellent results which can be expected from the consistent application of honesty and leading by example . . . my father.

INTRODUCTION

A changing of the guard is taking place within police departments across the nation. Every twenty-five years or so a generation of police administrators with experiences and philosophies rooted in the past retire, and younger middle management with new experiences and new philosophies move up the ladder to take the reins and to develop new programs, ideas, direction, and control of the organization.

Each operation is faced with new problems stemming from the natural social change. Each must also deal with unsolved problems from the previous era, and with issues that require fresher approaches, approaches which often conflict with the philosophies and tactics of predecessors.

In the 1930s or even 1950s, this changing of the guard had little impact on direction of police organizations or the solving of internal problems. Lumbering forward, the police continued to deal with day-to-day brush fires, entrenching the agencies into a reactive component of the criminal justice system.

A poorly educated and isolated police service existed in most communities until the socially tragic decade of the sixties. A close examination of police management and administration history reveals that the 1960s brought about the first widespread meaningful shake-up in police education and the first steps toward bridging the gap between the service and the community it serves.

The bridge has widened considerably since the sixties. Police have moved from organizational atrophy into an era of new awareness of how their overall mission fits into the scheme of contemporary society.

The seed of the police service's new awareness began in earnest sometime in the latter part of that decade. It has taken twenty years for that seed to germinate, causing a new generation of police managers to contend with the impact of more social change than the previous two eras combined. Many large agencies grasped the importance of change early, implemented changes, and now shine as models for others. Larger agencies are often forced to change more rapidly because they are saddled with wider representation within their management ranks. Often that representation includes the managers of tomorrow and, since advancement in larger agencies is more swift than in smaller agencies, new ideas, approaches, and programs arrive faster and meet less resistance.

Unfortunately, some current middle-level police managers see themselves in an administrative purgatory. Although they are in a position to affect meaningful change within their organization, they often meet political and internal resistance to new ideas, limiting their ultimate effectiveness. As the generational evolution continues, current middle-level managers will find themselves in a position to plan more long-term and meaningful change. An agenda for change is needed to focus the efforts of these managers on unified goals. First and foremost, we must develop a blueprint that is founded upon modern management science, not just police management techniques. The blueprint must blend the future of police service, community attitudes, factors which will affect crime in the future, and the people who will be responsible for getting the job done.

This book provides a route to a common agenda, a unified goal. Quick solutions will not be found, but every avenue, including approaches that may appear radical to some practitioners, will be explored.

Despite what some teachings would have us believe, management of a police organization bears a striking resemblance to management in private business. The principles are the same. It is time for police managers and administrators to cast aside much of the old tradition and work to blend the police service more harmoniously with today's society.

There are some fine police organizations in the United States. Unfortunately, others operate in spite of poor upper management and leadership. Those agencies are all plagued by a common denominator: failure to grasp, accept, and implement meaningful change.

Although there is no way to overhaul the police service overnight, futuristically-minded managers can begin to move forward on their own without waiting for social demands to force change. Staying ahead of society's mandatory changes and broadening perspectives through progressive programs will enhance any organization ... especially the police organization.

Where does it start? It starts with tackling problems in a no-nonsense style and by discarding the old taboos that isolate police agencies as organizational islands. It starts with managers removing themselves from the gamemanship and rules from previous management eras. It starts with researching issues discussed in this book with an open mind; not with the attitude of *we can't do that because it's never been done before.*

It starts with establishing a climate in which police officers can participate in the direction of their own organizations. It starts with senior management leading the way and teaching up-and-coming managers new ways to handle police-related problems without relying strictly upon formal power.

Some practitioners—those who are frozen into the philosophy that there is only one way of approaching any problem—will probably set this book aside. It is to be expected. It reflects the way some have managed in the past to make problems go away by not dealing with them. Many other practitioners may take issue with concepts and comments in the text. That is as it should be. Police managers need to examine, disagree, discuss, think of alternatives, and open their minds to new ideas.

Planners should keep in mind an axiom which has been used many times as an analogy for managers. There are no bad orchestras, only bad conductors . . .

The terms supervisor, manager, administrator, leader, and planner are used interchangeably and synonymously in this test.

ACKNOWLEDGMENTS

This book had its beginnings in the mid 1970s, although it was not realized at the time. During that period, my concerns about the limitations of police service originated and grew from the conditions under which law enforcement agencies operated at the time. Outdated policies and practices which imposed unnecessary strictures made it easy to identify the vast differences between academic theory and application. More disconcerting was learning that these differences were echoed even louder at the management and administrative levels and that many of the problems impede police service from era to era. Growth and experience validated this finding, and I developed a distinct appreciation of the extent and common causes of management atrophy in police organizations.

Diagnosing the ailments does not make the treatment a simple task. Prescriptions require that change take place in an organizational system that is too embedded with practices based upon tradition instead of innovation. Over the decades many prescriptions have been introduced and much has been written about the management practices of police organizations. Most of these studies and materials advanced the notion that the service needed to move away from the dependence on *gut feel* as a management style and to institute a more scientific foundation through which to achieve modern managerial behavior. Writings have offered the proper definitions, but have often fallen short in supplying practical mechanisms through which to move toward this goal.

The absence of a practical and useable framework that is in concurrence with contemporary issues facing police work has been a problem for the planner who will be handling these problems in addition to those handed down, well into the next century. This work is designed for those planners. The text provides an historical perspective which allows planners to better understand why police service is in the condition it is at this time in this era. It also focuses on what can be done now and in the 1990s to better prepare for the next century.

This is not an answer book. It is offered to provoke thought. It scratches the surface so to incite the planners who will need the vision to advance police service through the 1990s. The book should be read along with other modern management works which are available to innovative planners who are slowly becoming the majority in the field of law enforcement and criminal justice. There will be many other resources from which to draw upon as the 1990s pass. This text is intended as a contribution to the awakening of sound police management practices needed for the future of police service.

The transition of ideas into a published work requires a tremendous amount of support and encouragement. David Wilkinson provided both, as well as his time and direction and interest, for which I am grateful.

I have been fortunate to have developed friendships and associations with law enforcement managers throughout the country. Our exchanges of views and discussions on leadership and management have influenced me in my work and in the preparation of this book. My gratitude for many of these influences is extended to: Lawrence E. Walsh, Drexel T. Neal, Peter W. Anderson, Donald C. Whitham, Neal L. Brittain, William L. Tofoya, and Michael Duncan.

There are many other relationships which have influenced and reinforced positions I have taken on a variety of issues concerning police work, management, and simply dealing with people. These relationships have been tremendously important throughout my career and in my development as a manager. For these diversified influences, my deep appreciation is also extended to: Larry S. Roberts, William E. Burnett, Jr., Patrick H. Molloy, R.R. Phillips, Estella Mae Wilkinson, and the Millersburg Military Institute.

John Bizzack
Lexington, Kentucky

CONTENTS

POLICE MANAGEMENT FOR THE 1990s
A Practitioner's Road Map

Chapter 1

EVOLUTION AND INFLUENCES ON POLICE ORGANIZATION CULTURE

Police machinery in the United States has not kept pace with modern demands. It has developed no effective technique to master the burden which social and industrial conditions impose. Clinging to old traditions, bound by old practices which business and industry long ago discarded, employing some personnel poorly adapted to its purpose, it grinds away on its perfunctory task without self-criticism, without imagination, and with little initiative.[1]

An honest evaluation may lead you to think that this statement was made recently. Actually written in 1912, it was a part of a major study conducted by the Cleveland Foundation when it examined police service in Cleveland and other parts of the country.

In 1967, fifty-five years after the Cleveland Foundation Study, the President's Commission on Law Enforcement and the Administration of Justice reported this similar observation.

> Many police agencies are resistant to change. Police organizations frequently fail to determine shortcomings of existing practices through research and analysis. They are reluctant to experiment with alternative methods of solving problems. The police service must encourage, indeed put forth a premium, on innovation, research and analysis, self-criticism, experimentation and business management.[2]

Today, this statement is still uniquely applicable to many police organizations. The police service has always had its critics, but it is rare that an organizational culture repeats its mistakes so often.

To effectively determine where the police service needs to go, managers need to have some knowledge of where it has been. Some versions of police history leave the mistaken impression that technology alone has catapulted police service into the 21st century. Since police officers now have instant communication capabilities and computers at their disposal, it may appear that little is left to be done except to purchase more technology. This line of thinking is a modern reflection of past observations like those by the President's Commission and the Cleveland Foundation.

Regardless of history, a practitioner must understand that, as a whole, police service is still relatively undimensional when compared to other dynamic influences on society such as business and education.

HISTORICAL PERSPECTIVES

Today's police organization is rooted in a political and social struggle of the past. In Europe, most police organizations existed as an arm of a nation's or region's ruler. Police were rarely held accountable for their own actions, and preserving the status quo was their primary objective. Their tactics were rarely questioned as long as their results supported the regime.

Perhaps Britain's police force most closely parallels those which ultimately evolved in the United States, but their original mission, limited duties, and lack of true organizational structure led to controversial transformations in the mid-1700s.

Henry Fielding, an English Magistrate, published several papers on the police service around this time. Fielding's essential philosophy hinged on the goal of assuring swift and fair justice. The ongoing industrial revolution had brought about unforeseen social consequences such as hunger, disease, and widespread poverty. Inevitably, their newfound problems led to social violence and a new focus for police service.

After years of restructuring, Britain emerged with a consolidated police force made up of Irish constables, Scottish county police, and numerous small-town policemen. The reform called for a para-militarization of the civilian police force and a new system of discipline based on the relationship between leaders, men, morals, and militaristic-styled training. Britain's unifier force became the first police system based upon the concept of organization principles.

During this period, the trial-and-error approach to police administration and management prevailed. There were no strong philosophical principles to guide planners on police procedures. However, a strong military model did exist, and from this framework the police organization borrowed the first guidelines used to address direction, control, and bureaucracy.

At the same time in the United States, constables, whose duties were similar to those in Britain, were found in most townships and larger cities. Sheriffs were used in the counties. As cities grew larger in the east, more constables were hired, giving root to the traditional police mentality that still exists: when the population grows, hire more police; don't bother first improving the services that already exist.

As the west expanded, the sheriff became the chief law enforcement officer of the day. Early American societies, influenced by their European history, were very reticent about entrusting vast powers to their police forces. As a result, the sheriff's office was established as an elective position which assured some control while ultimately resulting in the office being void of a true law enforcement mission.[1]

From a professional standpoint, the constable of the day was not much better off than the sheriff. Constable positions were strictly appointive. Politics determined the nature of the service to be provided and who provided the service.

The municipal police agency evolved from the initial constable role, a night watch for most cities. Daytime policing actually began around 1800 and was borne out of necessity, not planning. Since most constables worked at night, most thieves began working during the day. New York City is commonly recognized as taking the lead in developing the twenty-four-hour police system. In 1844, New York's police department was authorized a strength of 800 men who were divided into a geographical precinct designed to **cover the clock.**

As the United States population shifted westward, other major cities began to introduce municipal policing, but the influence of politics, internal corruption, and the lack of a defined organizational mission retarded police service. As problems increased, the practice of increasing the size of the police force became recognized as the basic solution to all ills by administrators and politicians.

Political influence was the target of most cities in that era. Many reform movements were touted, but few caught on and most police organizations failed to adopt standards that would put some distance between the organization and the affects of politics on management.

Not until the economic crash of 1929 and the depression years that followed did police service discover the benefits of an educated police corp. Some notable and forward-thinking administrators surfaced prior to 1929, but their visions fell primarily on deaf ears.

In urban areas, where jobs were scarce, police service was seen as work that offered some security and a regular paycheck. More people competed for open positions, thus a better educated police officer emerged. Thoughts began to surface on the feasibility of a professional police corp.

Another era would pass before the validity of this thinking would be recognized.

A better educated police corp improved the stature of the job in the 1940s and 1950s, but old management principles, still deeply embedded, continued to plague police organizations. It was during this period that business and industry, already questioning their methods of management, adopted a more contemporary style.

Civil unrest and a more liberal Supreme Court drastically influenced police behavior and management in the 1960s. Felt strongly for a quarter century, it forced police organizations to change and further stiffened traditional resistance within police service.

Meanwhile, civil strife swiftly underscored the disjointed practices of police agencies. The police agency's traditional social isolation resulted in many managers failing to understand the causes and the ramifications of the social conflicts of the 1960s.

Television, of course, highlighted the ineptitude of the police in dealing with social conflict. Police were instantly cast on the evening news as oppressors and instruments of brutality. Violations of constitutional rights were headlines, and the police were caught in the cross-fire between status quo, as they had been taught, and the inevitability of change, which they resisted. An entire century of police management philosophy began to erode in a few short years. The police service was being boiled alive. It was time for a **nation wide** evaluation of the country's police corp.

A NEW ERA EMERGES

In 1967, President Johnson's Commission on Law Enforcement and the Administration of Justice examined the problem of crime and the police response to crime for the past forty years. Had it not been for the social upheaval in the 1960s, another decade or so may have passed before law enforcement drew such national scrutiny. For the first time, the study recognized police agencies as an essential component of the criminal justice system.

More than 200 recommendations were produced by the Commission in all areas of criminal justice, calling for basic changes in the operation of police agencies. But the Commission's findings carried no force of law; only public agreement or sentiment could induce the changes the Commission felt necessary. Larger police agencies adopted some recommendations and used the Commission's findings as leverage and argument for change. Many other police organizations were left puzzled by the findings, and most had inadequate funding to implement most recommended changes.

Politics again entered the playing field. Crime control was a major political issue in 1968 and, as a result, the Omnibus Crime Control and Safe Streets Act was enacted by Congress. The federal government's response to the issue was to pump millions of dollars into the criminal justice system and, at the same time, put some teeth into the Commission's recommendations. If state and local governments wanted to share the windfall of millions now available for law enforcement, they would have to adopt some sweeping changes.

As the first infusion of massive amounts of federal tax dollars dedicated to uniformly upgrading police service sifted downward, a new attitude within police administration began to emerge. This attitude became the forerunner of some of another ill-advised police management philosophy: money was the solution to all of the ills. Many productive programs were put into place during those years, and new technology made available through bountiful appropriations opened many doors. There is no question that this shot in the arm was necessary. The funding brought police service into the mainstream of the criminal justice system and demanded more accountability of law enforcement in general.

It also brought a recognized need for an educated police corp. Educational incentives were created and police officers began to pursue college hours and degrees. Many officers were for the first time exposed to certain academic concepts about management outside of police circles. Many officers hired during this era brought with them degrees in various fields which further heightened the awareness threshold of the overall police corp. Recruiting standards changed and higher education became a prerequisite for promotional considerations. **Professionalizing** law enforcement became a new crusade.

By 1978, the flood of federal monies was reduced to a trickle. Of course, the modest fiscal appropriations customarily allocated to underwrite police services by state and local governments were just not enough to continue all of the programs initiated under the 1968 Act.

Meanwhile, public attitudes had again changed direction and social upheaval and crime control were not of primary political importance. The millions consumed in funding special crime control programs, enhancing police technology, crime prevention, and investigations was seen as genuine advancement within the law enforcement branch of the criminal justice system, but the crime rate seemed unaffected.

During this period, the nation's economy struggled with the highest inflation rate of the century. Stretching the budget became the theme, and a turn toward social conservatism was observed. The economy was the political issue. Crime was still a concern, but it was popular for administrators to blame the economy on upswings in the crime rate. For the first time in American history, police agencies started laying off personnel. Police unions and the call for collective bargaining quickly followed. Police management was taxed from all sides. The brief **quick solution** period was over. It was time to remobilize, identify existing assets, and plan how police agencies could exist within the parameters of a changing society.

Thanks to a few forward-thinking police administrators who weathered this period, many agencies forged ahead while others returned to the comforts of isolation and a policy of reaction.

A major asset was easily identified from this era. It was estimated that over 30 percent of all of the police officers in the country had earned college degrees or had the equivalent of two years of college. It seemed likely that most of the officers who possessed formal educations were primarily found to be in the large to mid-size departments.

At no previous time in the history of police service could it be claimed that law enforcement was so well represented within the ranks of academia. Early theories contended that this was the primary legacy left by the federal money years, and many practitioners felt that a true **professionalism** standard was established. Educated, well-rounded officers proved to be more organizationally oriented and better understood their current role in society. The sociological blends required for human interaction from the police service were enhanced, but the police organization did not automatically become **professional**.

Similarly, broadened perspectives led to serious questioning of some police management traditions from within police ranks. A new generation of young officers more adept and sensitive toward community needs had become part of the corp. Evolving without a conscious plan became more objectionable to this newest era of police officer.

Critics outside police circles questioned the true value of a police corp formally educated in the relatively unproven science of **police administration.** Few disagreed with the need to increase educational standards in law enforcement, but others still agreed with the concept of continuing the isolation of police organizations by awarding degrees in fields that only presented the **police point of view** and lacked basic educational requirements of other disciplines. After all, law enforcement had just been pulled by the roots from decades of isolated practices. The primary concern of many was that the police would lapse back into that isolation.

Much of this criticism was unfounded. Higher education curriculums were broad enough in the various institutions of higher learning that offered degree programs in law enforcement science. However, little of what was instructed in the law enforcement field was fresh or innovative. Most instruction in police science courses focused on firearms, police history, criminal law, patrol techniques, and the basic requirements of being a policeman. Some organizational structuring was highlighted from texts written in the previous three decades. The fundamentals were taught, but one area was omitted: **modern** management and leadership.

Some officers who joined the ranks of the police corp in the 1970s had formal educations in other fields. Many others were veterans of the Vietnam conflict who brought with them still another form of **formal** education. These mixtures of attitudes, along with those of officers who were already police veterans and those from other varied backgrounds, set the tone for the future of police organizations: a blend of people representing a cross section of contemporary society. The most distinctive difference was that this era was less conservative and becoming more representative of contemporary society.

The officers of the 1970s are now becoming the police managers who will guide the police service into the final years of this century's decade. Their influence will be felt into the 21st century. A metamorphosis is taking place. The police service faces new problems but, more importantly, more police organizations are now consciously planning, moving from parochialism to a new awareness, actively defining police goals more precisely in order to meet existing demands and to anticipate future needs, acutely aware of social pressures, responding to marketing ideas, identifying political pressure, and studying the organization as a system. In essence, the police departments are becoming accountable to their communities.

ENDNOTES

1. Golver, Charles, A New Study of Police History. New York, Lover and Boyd, 1956, pp. 160–61.

2. President's Commission on Law Enforcement and the Administration of Justice, Task Force Report: The Police, Washington, D.C., U.S. Government Printing Office, 1967.

REFERENCES

Clift, Raymond E., *A Guide to Modern Police Thinking,* Cincinnati, Anderson, 2nd Edition, 1965.
Pascale, Richard Tanner, Zen and the Art of Management, N.Y., Wiley, Executive Success, Making it in Management, *Harvard Business Review,* 1983.

Chapter 2

CHANGE AND THE NEW ERA
OF POLICE MANAGEMENT

Despite continuous crises and brush fires that suddenly appear and require rapid responses, organizational change generally translates into gradual progress. Habit often has a stagnating effect on organizations by fostering a secure feeling that blinds people to the need for change. And although symptoms that identify needs for change are sometimes crystal clear, they are often ignored by those in positions of power. Clinging to old ways is more emotionally stable and comfortable. Whether fortunately or unfortunately, that approach is no longer adequate in operating modern police organizations.

All changes, even the minor ones, result in the disruption of familiarity. Change is mostly a psychological barrier from which the roots of resistance grow. People tend to repeat what works for them. A repeat of a formula that was successful in the past does not mean a formula is now in step with other changes that have taken place.

Two common conflicts are characteristic to all change. One comes from emotional attitudes of those affected by a change. Emotional conflict is usually based upon differences of opinion; facts rarely are the issue. The second is rational conflict which stems primarily from differences in people's values and experiences. When anticipating change, knowing which type of conflict may rise and how to deal with it will make the police manager more effective.

Conflict slows change. Both are inevitable and the police manager, just as any other manager, must resolve those conflicts to promote change effectively. Fear is usually cited as the number one reason for resistance to change in police organizations. Some may **fear** that they will lose power during a change. Some may **fear** that they will have to take on extra work or have less influence. Contrary to this short-sighted view, all people are found to **fear** the unknown—not just change. Fear of the unknown leads to the natural reaction of resistance because people

11

interpret change as forcing them to modify a comfortable habit. This, in turn, leads to another natural emotion: resentment. Resentment is usually aimed at those making the changes, because people feel they are being forced to alter safe habits without the opportunity to help plan the change or to have a voice in the original plan causing the change.

To alleviate the fear of the unknown and diffuse most opposition to change, contemporary police managers must look for ways to include their people in as many decisions as possible, then implement changes that are in the best interests of the organization and their people. Unfortunately, every decision to be made cannot be democratically achieved; some common sense must come into play. If change is going to affect familiar patterns or habits, the manager should develop a diffusion plan before making change; otherwise, it may be destined to be short-lived and ineffective.

Heavy-handed autocracy has usually been the method for police organizations implementing change. Modern practitioners agree that while autocratic management styles still have a place in organizations, the blend and extent of autocracy must be flavored with a dash of democratic consideration.

Nothing turns off the responsiveness of line staff to management as quickly as the autocrat. Many of the negative images and lack of progress which police have been saddled with since the turn of the last century may be directly traced to the autocratic management style. Stereotypically, police officers consider autocrats as the remnants from the days of lower recruitment standards: managers whose own insecurities are taken out on the rank and file. Fortunately, fewer truly autocratic police managers exist today, but those who do remain create obstacles that interfere with the advancement of sound management practices. There are still managers who ask themselves, **"How will this decision affect me,"** then make decisions based upon that personal perspective.

Fortunately, there are proven methods to introduce change at all levels of the police organization without turning out all of the old familiar habits. Practicing those methods in spite of entrenched autocrats is a skill that must be mastered by the new era of police managers. There are more officers today ready to accept change in order to make their jobs more effective and personally rewarding.

Usually, external environmental changes require police service to change habits in order to avoid catastrophes such as liability issues.

A large amount of change within police organizations over the past decade has been in response to, not in anticipation of, external changes. This sort of change action brings with it the classic patterns of **crisis management.**

Police organizations have much in common with the dead frog in the simple physiological experiment known as the boiled frog phenomenon. A frog is placed in a pan of cold water which is then heated on a burner. The heat is turned up gradually. As the heat increases, the frog sits in the pan and eventually boils to death. The change in the frog's cold water environment to the boiling water environment is so gradual that no response is triggered in the frog, thus the creature dies. If another frog is placed in a pan of water that is already boiling, that frog will not sit there, but will promptly jump out and survive. The experiment can continue to refine this procedure until it is discovered just how great the change in temperature has to be before the frog will respond. The boiled frog's threshold of awareness is set too high. Changes in the frog's environment lead to an undesirable consequence.[1]

Likewise, police management in the 1990s must set its threshold of awareness lower. Anticipation of environmental changes must set the stage for managers to plan, foresee conflict, diffuse opposition, and practice no-nonsense management. A no-nonsense method through which to introduce change is actually basic common sense, involving simple principles and requiring only that a manager talk to his subordinates. Police officers, like other workers, will accept most any change that is introduced to them if:

> ... the change is discussed with them as soon as possible and their ideas are solicited;
>
> ... the manager has all the facts that are needed to answer questions about the when, where, who, why, and how of the change;
>
> ... the manager stresses the positive aspects of the change and how the change will benefit them and the organization;
>
> ... the manager stays on the high road and refrains from downgrading past practices;
>
> ... the manager allows an adjustment period for the change to be adopted effectively;
>
> ... the manager follows up on the results of the change and provides feedback to subordinates on how the change has accomplished the intent.[2]

ORGANIZATIONAL CULTURES

Police managers could learn much by removing themselves from the closed circles of police science/administration for a moment and reflecting on how other organizations respond to change. For instance, American businesses have been forced over the past decade to closely reexamine the quality of their products. At one time, American business emphasized setting goals and controlling the organization, ultimately leading businesses into an era of the quick fix, sloppy thinking, and a cover-your-rear-end mentality. Enthusiasm slowly eroded the futuristic-minded manager. No reward was offered for imagination, commitment, or just plain knowing-how-to-handle-people. Management believed simply that the more the wages, the more productive the worker. Eventually, American businesses realized that money alone simply does not motivate people. Values had changed; there are other qualities sought in a job by the work force. For instance:

- a chance to think for themselves
- efficient managers
- an opportunity to see the end result of the work performed
- work that is not too easy and that is interesting
- association with other workers who treat each other with respect
- recognition for work that is well done
- an opportunity to present ideas on how to make the job more effective

Money and benefits are important to any worker, and those qualities cannot be ignored in a job; but contemporary managers must understand that money is not the primary motivator it used to be. Other, more useful motivators are ready and available.

American businesses use most of these motivators in one form or another to lure and/or retain the best people to their organizations. Police managers need to learn by watching American business and other organizations during periods of change like this. Is it possible for the bureaucratic structure of police organizations to adopt the distinctive changes that have taken place in other American businesses? Can the hierarchy be reduced? Can officers be given a common sense of purpose despite the lack of a real profit incentive? The answer is a resounding "Yes."

Police organizations have used every possible excuse when resisting change. Politics have been and still are one of the most worn excuses. Although politics do create external problems that lead to internal disruption, this excuse is one that is becoming less acceptable as politicians move toward changing police organizations into modern, responsive service organizations for their communities. Low pay has always been a popular excuse with the lament that police service cannot attract quality people, and the organization, therefore, is doomed to status quo existence. That excuse no longer holds water. Although pay has not increased dramatically for police officers, money has been proven to be less of a primary motivator for the modern worker. Meanwhile, many police organizations have claimed they could not change because they did not have enough equipment and technology. Although police budgets may leave a lot to be desired by the administrator, the problem is often not found in the amount of technology available, but knowing how best to use the technology that is available.

There is one excuse that has rarely been voiced from police administrators until recently. Unfortunately for the police organization, the **excuse** is being considered more of an actual cause of the traditional resistance to external and internal change: leadership style.

The leadership styles arising from the paramilitary structure of police organizations encourages autocracy. Coercive powers often stagnate meaningful growth and upward communications. That creates a negative impact which ultimately retards innovation within the police service and usually leads to withdrawal and alienation within the rank and file. This type of leadership style has worked against police organizations for the past several decades. The 1960s certainly shook the foundations of police organizations, but even that tragic period was not enough to loosen the grip of autocracy. The sad lessons are now being taught to yet another generation of managers. But more police managers today are recognizing the need to adjust to modern times. They see realistic limits on resources and more fully comprehend the true motivational factors influencing today's police officers.

Police managers from previous eras are exasperated with recommendations for modernizing police management in preparation for the 1990s and beyond. An unfortunate fact is that there are some police managers and administrators today who would join them.

Police managers of the 1990s will have to throw away some deeply embedded traditions and frames of reference they have witnessed in police management styles. There must be more risk-taking and a turnaround from the practice of making decisions that directly affect officers without soliciting their input. Organizations must reduce their reactionary reputation. Problems must be solved so that brush fires do not occupy all of the organization's resources and all of the manager's time. Autocratic styles must be used only when the situation demands that style, not as a cushion to fall back on when things are not going as planned. Managers must listen more carefully. The search for ideas must continue from the bottom up, not just from the top down.

LEADERSHIP DEVELOPMENT

Basic definitions of leadership, as defined in police circles, are picked up by future supervisors as soon as they begin preparations for competitive examinations. These definitions are standard in most testing for advancement. Recently promoted supervisors can easily grasp definitive characteristics and relate them to their new positions. The definition usually goes something like this: **Leadership is the process of influencing members of the organization to use their energies willingly and appropriately to facilitate the achievement of the police department's goals.**[3] When repeated before an oral board, this rote definition guarantees high marks for the candidate. But serious analysis of this can broaden the candidate's grasp of this basic tenement. For instance, the word **willingly,** an integral component of this definition, underscores that **influencing** is not a coercive act as would generally be the case in an autocracy. Candidates and current police managers also must grasp another powerful element that comes with rank advancement: once a person has entered a leadership position, he can never not lead. Why? No matter how right or wrong, every action influences others. Once formal power has been given, every decision and course of action taken by that person affects the organizational climate. In short, leaders affect the organization not only by what they do, but also by what they do not do.

A gap has always existed between academic theories of leadership and the everyday practice. Police organizations are increasingly willing to adhere to the practice of promoting people based on an assessment or testing situation, then to let those people learn as they go, a rather harsh on-the-job-training experience. As a result, many newly promoted supervisors quickly return to a greater dependence on their formal power, and they adopt the proven autocratic style. In the long run, this type of supervisory development undermines to the organization. It makes no more sense than giving a written test to a medical student, anointing him with the title of Doctor, and then escorting him into a surgery room to perform a major operation. There is simply more to it than passing a test; that's the easy part. Seldom does that person display the aptitude to apply that tested knowledge successfully. As a result, police leadership development gets started off on the wrong foot. This problem needs to be rectified before reevaluations of how middle management and executives are developed can be effective. As in all organizations, there are supervisors who rise through the ranks of midlevel management and into the executive or administrative levels without long-lasting side effects of this substandard, preliminary conditioning. There are the leaders who earn informal power and find it relatively simple to manage subordinates in their respective functions. These leaders, however, often see their effectiveness as being limited within the organizational structure as a whole. Although they manage their area with great success, other areas remain influenced by managers relying on the formal autocratic power of their rank. Inevitably, this situation leads to a few areas of a police organization being managed properly and other areas remaining static. The entire organization becomes off-balance. Too many leadership styles exist because there was no formal process through which to instill the same basic philosophies and approaches, and even less emphasis on continual supervisory evaluation and development.

Many police agencies promote staff members and immediately place them in positions of authority. When a supervisory school becomes available, those individuals may be fortunate enough to attend a forty-hour session. In some agencies, one supervisory course is all that is required after a promotion. The courses traditionally cover definitions, how to praise, how to discipline, performance appraisals, and some concepts of decision making. Practically every course is designed with the police organizational setting in mind. This instruction, coupled with what may have been retained from studying for the promotional test or assessment, is most frequently the total formal supervisory training a newly promoted police sergeant will receive or can hope for from an agency.

It is little wonder that by the time these people advance in rank, their exposure to how organizations work is one-dimensional. Police service does not permit lateral entry at any level other than chief. New ideas, concepts, and fresh attitudes must come from within. Portable pensions and lateral entry would be one solution to leadership stagnation at various levels, but other solutions must be sought.

Law enforcement is big business in today's economy. Police agencies rank as high, if not higher, than fire and public works in terms of demands on the tax dollars of most communities. It is not unusual to find a police agency serving a population of over 200,000 with a budget of $15 to $18 million. A rational citizen looking at a multimillion dollar business would expect the most administratively competent personnel to lead this major corporation, the local police agency. Unfortunately, that is not necessarily so.[4]

UNDERSTANDING TRUE PROFESSIONALISM AND THE DESIRE FOR RECOGNITION

When professionalism of and in police service is discussed, many definitions surface. The debate as to whether police service is a profession usually depends on where one stands. It is time that police service collectively identify the true meaning and application of the term in relationship to law enforcement. At this time, there is no clear definition of police professionalism that is applicable to all factions of law enforcement. Many police agencies refer to themselves as professionals, but when the term is applied in its generally accepted meaning, law enforcement's credibility suffers. **Webster's Encyclopedic Dictionary** assures that professionalism is **a calling superior to a mere trade or handicraft.** Police work is certainly beyond that of a trade or handicraft, but does that make it a profession in the eyes of society? Not at all. Professionalism is accompanied by formal power that comes with rank. Informal power, however, must be acquired by the leader through consistency, visibility, long-term integrity, and maintaining performance. It must be earned through application of the principles which support and demonstrate that a leader is capable of dealing with power.[5] Informal power, like professionalism, has to be earned; it cannot be anointed. Too often, those in police service appear to want the title without paying the price attached to it. Paying that price takes time. The 1990s, however, may be the catalyst for arriving at this final definition and understanding.

In general, professions may be categorized into three broad divisions: (1) scientific, (2) literary, and (3) social.[6] If police service fits into this division, then the latter would serve as their defined grouping. Society has long considered a profession to be defined by characteristics which are conspicuously absent in modern-day police service:

1. relative autonomy
2. public status and esteem
3. high requirements of abstract knowledge and higher educational aims
4. a viable organization or association central to the field
5. a governing code of ethics
6. mobility for its members
7. a strong service orientation[7]

Number seven is the only characteristic that legitimately links any aspect of professionalism with police service. In and by itself, one characteristic is not enough to justify defining the police service as a true profession.

There can never be autonomy in police work; it demands community involvement. Public status and esteem for police organizations vacillate tremendously. There are no high requirements of abstract knowledge nor higher educational aims when compared to true professions. There are some associations central to the field of law enforcement, but none represent all officers in the same manner that a medical society or a bar association represents its members. A code of ethics is touted by law enforcement officials, but it has no self-governing capacity, and it does not actually regulate the conduct of police officers. Civil service prevents mobility for members of the police service. Most police officers, regardless of rank, are restricted to one agency for an entire career if they are to recognize benefits of their pensions.[8]

On the other hand, there is one major element that sets law enforcement apart from all other organizations: discretionary power. This discretionary power reflects the attitudes of the community. If a community demands tough enforcement, they usually get it from the police. If they want to lessen the enforcement emphasis in a particular area, that usually comes about through the same pressures.

Before a collective plan can be identified to move the police service toward any degree of what society will accept as a profession, planners should consider the fact that there are over 17,000 police departments in the United States, employing around 480,000 officers.[9] More than 10,000 of these departments are estimated to employ less than nine sworn officers. Every police department will continue to be a representation of its individual community. In short, there can never be central and uniform professionalization.

Another area that needs special attention is overall police image and its influences on professionalism. Raymond Clift in his 1965 book, **A Guide to Modern Police Thinking,** called this area of concern **growing pains.** He contended that these **growing pains** were both positive and negative in their influences on how society felt about police service. Clift outlined four problems experienced by police agencies which made up these **growing pains.**

1. Public criticism of one department by another of the **dirty linen** washed in public because of this action.
2. Illegal investigative methods, which Clift contended were rare, but as long as they existed would receive prominence in the media and be a detriment to the good police work.
3. Favoritism in enforcement practices.
4. Collection of gratuities or **hand outs** to police by citizens.

Obviously, each of these areas affects the way society views police service, but planners realize there are more than four categories of growing pains which influence public sentiment in today's society. Clift's observations were sound in the 1960s, but they need to be expanded for the 1990s.

Clift's book rethought many of the old police practices, and forward-thinking practitioners were a minority when his first edition was published in 1956. When examining the various aspects of moving the police service towards professionalism, planners should keep in mind another of Clift's contentions. He did not feel it was unreasonable to expect that police would attain the rank of a profession in **another decade or so.**[20] That was in 1956. Police service has made its strides, but professionalism is a mantle which will absorb more time than Clift and many other police managers thought or may think.

Most practitioners agree that defining professionalism for the police corp, then coming up with a nationally acceptable plan that will not decrease community involvement, may be the right therapy for the long-suffered pains and atrophy in police management.

If there has ever been a proper time in history for police service to initiate that action, it is now. The awareness of this fundamental need is recognized by the majority in the police corp. This era represents the most educated police managers in history. External change factors have created the proper climate for this massive undertaking, and political waters are set at the correct temperature to entice this change. Planners should start to consider in earnest what vital areas need to be addressed in order for the police service to be true representatives of their community, yet uniformed and centralized in their mission and organizational standards.

If the police service is injected with the fuels and impetus for change, what issues, programs, and future concerns will planners have to anticipate as this century comes to a close? The process is going to take more than books to incite interest of this magnitude. It will take more than articles in trade journals to instill the concepts and plant the seeds of change. It will take the rest of this era and much of the next to effectively transform police service. The momentum is building slowly. Managers are marshalling attitudes and building more productive and futuristically-minded programs within their agencies. These programs are the core of change, the very center of the centrifugal force that will ultimately shift police work into a higher gear.

Once the organizational clutch is fully released, the gears can be shifted with less energy. The next generation of police managers will be responsible for again switching those gears at the proper time in order to anticipate and adapt to the inevitability of changes in society. Police managers in the 1990s should view themselves as mechanics. It is their responsibility over the next decade to assure their agency's transmission is fully compatible with the clutch and shifting gears.

ENDNOTES

1. Tichy, Noel M., Davanna, Mary Ann, The Transformational Leader, N.Y., Wiley and Sons, 1986, p. 44.
2. Standards Manual for Supervisors, Bureau of Business Practices, Prentice Hall, Waterford, 1987, 3rd. p. 20.
3. Swanson, Charles R., Territo, Leonard, Police Administration, N.Y., McMillan, 1983, p. 97.
4. Thibault, Edward A., Lynch, Lawrence M., McBride, R. Bruce, Proactive Police Management, Englewood Cliffs, Prentice-Hall, 1985, p. 49.
5. Lynch, Ronald G., The Police Manager, 3rd, N.Y., Random House, 1986, p. 153.
6. Clift, Raymond E., A Guide to Modern Police Thinking, 2nd, Cincinnati, 1965, p. 326.
7. Eastham, George D., Municipal Police Administration, Washington, D.C., International City Managers Association, 1971, pp. 332–45.

8. Swanson, Charles R., Territo, Leonard, Police Administration, N.Y., Macmillan, 1983, p. 99.
9. Vaughn, Jerald R., Presentation in new Orleans, Drug Control Strategy Conference, April 1987.
10. Clift, Raymond E., A Guide to Modern Police Thinking, 2nd, Cincinnati, 1956, p. 331.

REFERENCES

Quality Leadership: The First Step Towards Quality Policing, Couper, David C., Lobitz, Sabine H., *The Police Chief,* April 1988.

Excellence in Policing: Models for High Performance Police Organizations, Brown, Lee P., *The Police Chief,* April 1988.

The Police Manager, Lynch, Ronald G., Random House, N.Y., 1986, 3rd.

Chapter 3

CHALLENGING THE FOUNDATIONS
OF POLICE ORGANIZATION:
A LOOK AT THE FUTURE

The police service cannot prepare for the future without taking into consideration current trends in crime and evaluating what implications those trends will have in the future. Impressive studies have taken place in recent years. Yet, many of the prognostications stemming from these studies are viewed with a jaundiced eye by police managers who still find it difficult to plan in a synergistic style or to look at the big picture. The study of the future is often reduced to the traditional reactionary approach by police planners, and rarely is a connection between problems and their underlying causes sought. Issues of the day are easily categorized. The issues are basically the same ones upon which the media focuses their attention; drugs, domestic violence, child abuse, terrorism, pornography, the fundamental fear of violent crime, and property thefts.[1]

In the grandest tradition of feeling comfortable and content with existing technological capabilities, some police agencies boast that recent introductions and use of computers are the answer to crime control. There is merit to this concept, and the most recent survey of computerization in law enforcement does reflect that most of the police agencies in the United States which serve a population of 50,000 or more have some computer capability. However, another survey dims this bright star. Analysts with the International Association of Chiefs of Police estimate that only 10 percent of these departments use their computers in imaginative ways. Most of their new-found technology is used for electronic storage only.[2]

Before exploring forecasts, police managers should be reminded of the two principles which influence police service. A brief familiarization of earlier era philosophies and their founders may be quite helpful for planners aiming to more objectively understand their influences and attitudes toward forecasts.

BASIC PHILOSOPHIES OF POLICE SERVICE

August Vollmer was police chief for thirty years in Berkeley, California. His legacy is the crusade he led for reformations of police service through technology and higher personnel standards. His department was the first to encourage higher education of its members, to modernize records, to develop beat allocation analysis, and to reduce political appointments within the organization by establishing a solid merit and performance standard for advancements. Vollmer also must be accredited with setting up the first scientific crime laboratory in the United States and introducing polygraph into criminal investigation. His tenure at Berkeley from 1902 through 1932 transformed that police department into a model.

Vollmer produced another recognized leader of early police reform, O.W. Wilson. Practically every police manager of the past twenty-five years has been exposed to the police administration texts written by Wilson, and most departments are still fundamentally set up under his concepts of how a police organization should be run. Wilson's influence was first felt at Wichita, Kansas. Wilson, who had been an officer in the Berkeley Police Department, was assisted by Vollmer in gaining this appointment.[3] His eleven years in that city as police chief, then another twenty years as Dean of the School of Criminology in Berkeley, helped change the climate of police administration in the early part of this century. From 1960 to 1967, Wilson was Superintendent of the Chicago Police Department where his reform efforts became legendary.[4]

Both Vollmer and Wilson are identified as proponents of the social service philosophy in law enforcement, better known today as **problem-oriented policing**. The philosophy encouraged by Vollmer and Wilson view police as **criminologists** who must deal with the problems of crime and criminal behavior at the community level. Crime prevention, community relations, and community involvement programs all stem from this philosophy.[5]

There is another philosophy existing today whose roots grew from the models left by two other police administrators of early eras. J. Edgar Hoover's **legalistic philosophy** emphasized law enforcement only as the key to successful policing. Social service involvement by the police is practically nonexistent under this philosophy. William H. Parker, former chief of the Los Angeles Police Department, shared this view, and the influence of his and Hoover's organizational approaches led many police managers into taking the **hard line** approach to policing. Usually a blend of the two philosophies is observed across the country, but a shift is being recognized towards the science of Vollmer's and Wilson's ideas.

Fewer police managers today subscribe to the assumption that the best way to control crime is to jail criminals. As a true modern police manager knows, there is no one best way to do anything, much less to deal with crime. Jailing criminals is effective in most instances, but contemporary society requires a more synoptic approach to this philosophy. One alternative is to identify solutions and match them to the problems, help potential crime victims find ways to protect themselves, and reduce the opportunity for crime.

Current practitioners use one or the other of these philosophies to establish the tone of their agency. There are situations arising from external environmental changes that often require shifts back and forth until a blend is found that appears in line with the community. Those agencies failing to adjust, or to shift, have often lost touch with their communities, allowing the old isolation factors start to take hold again, and police service rapidly falls behind the times for another portion of an era.

PREDICTIONS AND FORECASTS

In 1987, Georgette Bennette's book, *Crimewarps, The Future of Crime in America,* became a bestseller. A former NBC correspondent, recognized criminologist, and widely published journalist, Bennette paints a picture of what crime patterns will evolve over the next fifty years. Her research produced forecasts that must be considered by every police manager. The book is controversial. Some outside the circles of law enforcement see the crime trends as unlikely occurrences. Some law enforcement practitioners also view the analysis with reservation, but this reaction is to be expected in the existing climate. Bennette's insights about justice and crime are in sync with other research prepared by contemporary police administrators who are committed to the approach of problem-oriented policing. William L. Tafoya, a faculty member of the Behavioral Science Instruction and Research Unit at the FBI National Academy, prepared an even more detailed list of forecasts in 1987 which not only addressed the police service specifically, but was so bold as to forecast the year in which those changes will take place. Tafoya is a Supervisory Special Agent with the FBI and based his findings on a major study done by eight scholars and seven law enforcement executive representatives of the nation's law enforcement management experts.

There are other sources, studies, and articles which relate to the topic, but these two closely translate into the type of language more apt to be appreciated and understood by a police service which is predictably reticent to accept the consequences of failing to plan.

Dr. Bennette's insights into justice and crime translate into a true sociological examination of what may take place in the United States over the next few decades. The term crimewarp is one she coined to describe the bends in today's trends that will affect the way people live tomorrow. There are six crimewarps influenced by what Dr. Bennette claims to be major social transformations. She recognizes and shows that crime is not static. Unfortunately, law enforcement organizations have just begun to realize this, as seen in their recent attempts to handle new types of crimes which have resulted from fast-changing society. The crimewarps examined explain crime and its influence on society's thinking; from total fear to genuine, obsessive fascination. To understand the fluency of the forecast in Crimewarps, a planner must read and analyze carefully. Bennette shows through her explanation of each crimewarp why the forecast has an extremely high probability of occurring. This chapter will only outline the six crimewarps so that police managers will be exposed to sampling of the perceptive analysis offered in Bennette's book. The illustrations should make all police managers think a little more about the future and how frightening the future can be if the same techniques and measures, so trite within police service, are allowed to continue unchallenged.

SOCIETY'S CRIMEWARPS

Crimewarp 1: The New Criminals. Traditional criminals—young, male, poor, uneducated—will increasingly be displaced by older, more upscale offenders. The number of crimes committed by women will accelerate, not only in stereotyped areas like prostitution, but in white collar crime and domestic violence. Teenagers will commit fewer, but more terrible crimes. Senior citizens will enter the crime scene as geriatric delinquents.

Crimewarp 2: The March of Crime. Crime will become freer of geography. Less of it will take place at the neighborhood level. Where crime is spatially bound, it will shift from the Northeast to the Sunbelt and into rural areas.

Crimewarp 3: Ring Around the White Collar. The street crimes that scare us will decrease in relation to more impersonal, far-reaching white collar crimes. Computers, cashless money, and technological secrets will become the new booty. Patterns of consumer fraud will mold themselves around changed demographics, and we will find new ways of cheating old institutions.

Crimewarp 4: The Politics of Pleasure. Despite deeply rooted Puritan ethic and its contemporary expression in the New Right, some consensual crimes—drug abuse, homosexuality, prostitution, gambling—will be legalized. Others, like pornography, will be subject to stricter regulation.

Crimewarp 5: The Ups and Downs of Big Brother. Long entrenched crime fighting strategies will be displaced by leaner, more focused, less personal tactics. Efficiency and coverage will be enhanced by the proliferation of computers and high-tech listening/detection devices. Self-help, security hardware, and private police will reduce the reliance on traditional law enforcement. New architectural designs will build crime proofing into the environment.

Crimewarp 6: Paying the Tab for the Bill of Rights. Some of our civil liberties will be displaced in an effort to stem crime and the moral anarchy that underlies it. The erosion will occur in the process of deeding our privacy to computer files and our moral judgment to ultraconservatives.

Dr. Bennette summarizes the crimewarps as displacements in crime patterns. She explains how people often look at crime as something alien, but that it is actually a form of behavior that reflects a myriad of intersecting forces like economics, politics, religion, education, biology, law, values, and social forces within demographics. Appropriately, she points out that crime is a result of a breakdown in social controls and that it provides a mirror in which we can view how society functions.[6]

It is doubtful if the crimewarps will be widely accepted within most police circles. Although Dr. Bennette's forecasts are completely understandable, they do not incite overall police service agreement. Crimewarps do serve, however, to set the tone for the direction of crime in the future, as seen by most planners who will be directing police services in the 1990s.

In 1985, an exploratory field study was conducted through a method-

ological tool known as the Delphi technique. An anonymous, four itera-
tion mail questionnaire was initially used. The first phase of the study
called for a group of law enforcement specialists and experts to identify
topical areas viewed as vital to the future of law enforcement. The
following three iterations were comprised of forced-choice items which
were used to extract the opinion of the specialist concerning the topics
and issues presented. Twenty-five issues and topics, grouped into six
clusters, surfaced: traditional crime, pervasive crime, high technology,
alternative policing, professionalization, and research. A consensus was
reached by the specialists on seventeen of the twenty-five items (68
percent). William L. Tafoya summarized the study through the publication of research findings in an essay appearing in Law Enforcement
Technology magazine entitled, Into the Future...A Look at the 21st
Century.[7] The information specifically focuses on what role police will
play in the 1990s up through the year 2050. The data is more likely to be
acceptable to police planners because it relates directly to the police role.
Planners who know and understand how police service evolved to its
present day era, and who grasp the necessity of designing a blueprint for
the 1990s, will discover that Tofoya's summarization of the Delphi forecasts brings disheartening news, but a highly probable timetable under
which police service will attain the status of a true profession. It will be
disappointing to many law enforcement agencies to see that true professionalism will escape the current and most likely the next two generations of police service, but it will take place because of **change** in the way
police service will respond to crime problems in the future. Of course,
the **changes** will be a result of avenues taken by the police managers and
planners of the 1990s. Tofoya aptly points out in his essay that police
service will be compelled to endure the future if planners do not shape
its course.

Planners should analyze the following forecasts in perspective with
their own jurisdictions, as well as the national scene. This convergence
will permit a more appreciable understanding and complete overview of
the predictions, affording a planner with the insight necessary to translate alternative planning into viable courses of action for their agency.

FORECASTS FOR POLICE SERVICE

1990: A significant increase in the enforcement of law related to
both violent crime and property crime will be observed. The legalistic

style of policing will reach its zenith in the next four years. As law enforcement focuses its attention on the traditional crimes—those with which it is equipped to deal and understand—computer related crime will emerge as a threat to economic and national security. What may appear as a sudden increase in computer crime will actually be a result of what has grown steadily over the previous decade, but was largely ignored.

1995: Law Enforcement can expect a temporary respite. The involvement of the average citizen in policing will become the norm. This is expected to relieve law enforcement of some of the burden carried since the emergency of the professional model of policing. The acceptance of community involvement by law enforcement will signal the shift from a legalistic style to a service oriented philosophy as the dominant style of policing. The metamorphosis can be attributed to present day university and professionally conducted research. Research will begin to be utilized to a much greater degree in establishing crime reduction strategies than has been the case in the past.

Terrorism will emerge as a major problem in the United States by 1995. Much of this may be attributed to externally-oriented retaliations stemming from the United States' involvement in the affairs of other nations. Right-wing militancy should not be discounted, fueled by perceived injustices by the liberal factions of America.

1997: State-of-the-art high technology may begin to be employed in combatting crime; however, the high technology will not necessarily be employed to deal with sophisticated crime. The new strategies are more likely to be used to deal primarily with more traditional crimes.

1999: Massive urban unrest and civil disorder is expected to plague America as it did two decades ago. The trigger mechanism could be a reaction to the intensified law enforcement efforts expected by 1990. It is more likely, however, to stem from acerbic social conditions. If the economy continues to falter, the catalyst for calamity could result from massive frustration over conditions of chronic low wages or no wages. Together with the widespread perception of unfair foreign competition and a seemingly intransigent federal posture, volatile turbulence lacks but a spark.

2000: Local law enforcement could be overwhelmed by sophisticated crime and may be reduced to taking preliminary reports.

Short-sighted administrators and the inadequate technical skills of investigators today provide a clue as to what tomorrow may bring. Despite whatever use of high tech might be made in 1997, it will likely not be enough and may be too late.

To compound law enforcement's problems, the shortcomings of computerized files recognized today will probably go largely uncorrected. Thus, by the year 2000, it is expected that such systems will become the target of legal action. Further, inadequacies and inaccuracies are expected to be so pervasive that the majority of the lawsuits are likely to be won by well-prepared plaintiffs.

Computer-based instruction (CBI) is expected to become the standard for training in law enforcement by the year 2000. Because of the phenomenon of time lag, CBI is unlikely to have any significant effect on the incidence of computer-related high tech crime or computer-related-legal challenges. The impact should be felt from this training five to ten years later.

2005: By this year, it is expected that events of the previous two decades, more vigorous enforcement of traditional crime laws, an increase in computer-related crime (largely a crime of the upwardly mobile elements of society), university/professional research, and urban unrest will lead to the identification of economic deprivation as the major factor with regard to the incidence of traditional crime. The occurrence of this forecast will result in research playing a major, but not pivotal, role. The increased incidence of competent research, examining various aspects of community involvement in policing, and expected civil unrest, for example, may yield unexpected findings that point to economic deprivation as the cause of crime. Policy makers, however, must still deal with such issues.

2025: By this year, the majority of all law enforcement executives can be expected to have changed their leadership style to reflect a proactive goal orientation. The traditional autocrative management philosophy is expected to be largely abandoned. In part, this could come about because of the impressive number (but still a minority) of highly educated law enforcement administrators today. As their ranks grow, they will come to recognize that highly motivated personnel need guidance and support, not threats of action and stricture. It will also be facilitated, however, by the simultaneous emergence (by 2025) of a formal education as the standard for entry and advancement in law enforcement. If one forecast holds, the other is expected as well. If one falls short or fails to materialize, so then will the other. The events leading to these two forecasts are expected to share a symbolic relationship. Thus, we are likely to see both forecasts, but not either alone.

2035: By this year, it is expected that private security agencies will assume a significant role of all law enforcement responsibilities. Given the number of events that are expected to precede this one, there are a variety of factors that could contribute to private security/police cooperative ventures. The most plausible single factor, however, is likely to be economics of scale. A protracted downturn in the economy could force such a merger or, in the worst case, bring about total and complete police privatization.

A less pessimistic perspective suggests that insight may be gained from the combination of greater citizen involvement in policing and university/professional research (both expected to emerge forty years earlier, by 1995). Both may suggest areas in which it will benefit local law enforcement to have private security perform certain tasks for which they are now responsible. The use of cadets, dispatchers, reserves, meter maids, crossing guards, and other paraprofessionals has long been an accepted practice in law enforcement. In principle, there seems little difference between the use of such nonsworn individuals and the use of private security personnel.

2050: By this mid-century mark, the long awaited mantle of professionalism is expected to be bestowed on law enforcement. Seven factors are likely to contribute to this.

1. The movement toward accreditation of law enforcement agencies today.
2. The incorporation of university and professional research in the development of crime reduction strategies (fifty-five years earlier, by 1995) can be expected to cause police to become more objective and analytical in their outlook toward crime and criminals.
3. The standardization of CBI (a half century earlier, by 2000) can be expected to exemplify greater consistency and more clearly articulate goals and objectives in the development of training materials and programs.
4. The standardization of a formal education for entry and advancement (twenty-five years earlier, by 2025) should bring about not only more analytical and better informed police officers, but may also bring about more tolerant attitudes. College educated police

officers can be expected to view the citizens with whom they inter-
act as clients and patients rather than the enemy.

5. Enlightened leadership cannot help but advance the cause of
professionalism. Not only can the emergence of proactive and
goal-oriented leaders (quarter century earlier, by 2025) be expected
to be more analytical, objective and innovative, but tolerant as
well.

6. To a lesser degree, citizen involvement is expected to emerge
fifty-five years earlier (by 1995).

7. The greater involvement of private security, expected to emerge
fifteen years earlier (by 2035), may help the move toward a general
public acceptance of law enforcement as a profession. Because a
large number of citizens are expected to have been actively involved
in policing over such a long period of time, they should come to
recognize the dramatic difference between policing on television
and on the streets. More importantly, the public should come to
understand the difficulty and complexity of the responsibilities of
law enforcement officers. The average citizen is expected to develop
an awareness of what is best handled by **professionals.** The utiliza-
tion of private security may serve such a purpose as well. By the
year 2050, the public and the police themselves are expected to
understand the meaning of professionalism.

The simultaneous emergence (by 2050) of strong empirical research
capabilities in more than half the nation's law enforcement agencies can
be expected. The two major contributory factors will be the long-term,
regular exposure to competent researchers and research, and their own
formal education. The exposure to and involvement with scholars and
professional researchers directing action research in their agencies (for
about fifty-five years) should provide a nurturing environment and
mentoring relationship for law enforcement which can be expected to
become assimilated nationwide. The standardization of formal education (by 2025), before the advent of professionalism, implies that an
entire generation of law enforcement officers should cease being derided
or ridiculed because of their education. A college education is expected
to be the norm, then, as should be the desire and ability to test assump-
tions and experiment with new methods and procedures.

ENDNOTES

1. Tofoya, William I., Into the Future, A Look at the 21st Century, N.Y., *Law Enforcement Technology Magazine,* September/October 1987.
2. Ibid.
3. Bopp, William J., *Crisis in Police Administration,* Springfield, Thomas, 1986, pp. 106–12.
4. Ibid., p. 157.
5. Ibid., p. 157.
6. Bennette, Georgette, *Crimewarps, The Future of Crime in America,* N.Y., Anchor/Doubleday, 1988, Reprinted with permission.
7. Tofoya, William I., Into the Future, A Look at the 21st Century, N.Y., *Law Enforcement Technology Magazine,* September/October 1987, Reprinted with permission. Copyright by Media Horizons, Inc., 1987.

Chapter 4

A PRACTITIONER'S ROAD MAP
FOR THE FUTURE

P ractically every book published on the topic of police administration
or the police service reserves a chapter to address the future. Readers
are dealt a plethora of qualities that future leaders must demonstrate in
order for the police organization to survive. For the most part, the
recommendations are noteworthy. They are needed and they should be
read, understood, and absorbed into the daily practices of police management. However, a more aggressive stance is needed. Today's police
planners need an outline, a road map of sorts. What has worked in other
agencies? Why has it worked? How does it fit into the forecasts outlined
in the preceding chapter? What synoptic programs exist for the various
size departments in this country? What will this road map do for the
community and police service?

This chapter contains such a map. Disagreement as to the worth of the
map is inevitable. Disagreement in this form is healthy for organizations;
it will force managers to start thinking collectively, with the big picture
in mind. This map is not offered as a representation of what must take
place over the next decade, and it is certainly not all inclusive. But the
map does serve as a mechanism to generate ideas for planners and
practitioners in the 1990s.

ESSENTIAL AREA OF CHANGE—THE LEGEND

If true change is to be facilitated in the 1990s, there are two essential
areas which must serve as the legend to this map. Breaking this ground
will expedite the quest of police service to declare itself in concert with
modern management science.

The first essential is to redefine the need for developing future police
leadership. Currently, no true systematic plan exists to uniformly develop
police leadership across the country. Limiting selection to managers

within a police department isolates and stagnates police service thinking. The absence of a system increases the abundance of police managers who are less willing to introduce change or become agents of change within their own agencies. Traditionally, the only externally trained individuals welcomed in the police service are new police chiefs. In some instances, this singular change at the top provides enough impetus to induce progressiveness; but, as pointed out earlier in this text, change must come from both the top and bottom of an organization, not just the top. Lateral entry at management levels injects new influences required to facilitate an overall change. Of course, there are progressive practitioners who can initiate meaningful change if they are promoted from within their own department, but we should again examine the American business experience. Where would business be if there were not lateral external movements up and down the organization?

To accomplish lateral entry, portable pensions would be necessary. Nationally accepted standards of education, training, or experience should be adopted. The concept does not come without built-in bureaucratic obstacles, but that's what managers are for, to melt and remove obstacles. A plan is needed now.

The second essential of the map legend can be defined as the development of untapped resources within the police organization: simple employee relations. Former FBI Director Clarence M. Kelly emphasized that the need to instill an attitude which encourages creativity and innovative thinking cannot be ignored and that leaders need to encourage a perception of change as part of the thinking process of every officer on a daily basis. This simply means that a greater responsiveness must be demonstrated by police managers to the ever-changing needs of their employees. Participative and interactive management would go a long way in attaining this climate for change within many organizations. A more effective process to assure that officers' skills are appropriately matched with their interests and the goals of the organization would also advance the relationship between police management and police officers. This part of the legend should represent police management's responsibility to keep in mind that the old managerial concepts of years past do not always work effectively in today's environment. People perform effectively and productively when management allows them to obtain optimum personality expression while at work.[1] Once again, the concept does not come without built-in obstacles, primarily from the bureaucratic, paramilitary structure of police organizations, but managers must not let what they can't do interfere with what they can do when it comes down to this one-on-one essential. The principles of interactive management basically require face-to-face contact, getting out of the office or car, talking to the people getting the job done, listening, and promoting expression. Managers can do that regardless of department-wide obstacles with which they may currently disagree.

USING THE MAP

Maps most frequently are used to present explorers, travelers, or the lost with an overview of a region with which they are not completely familiar. Police management falls into each of those categories of users. There are many programs across the country which are deserving of a reference on any police planner's map. Most criminal justice and law enforcement periodicals, newsletters, and bulletins are full of new approaches being used in the United States by a cross section of police and criminal justice agencies. Many departments pick up new ideas from these sources, rearrange them to fit neatly into their budgets and community needs, put them into effect, and wait for the next publication. Some agencies may struggle with the undertaking and never quite get it off the ground, or find that adopting too many programs too quickly is more than their agency can handle. There is nothing wrong with this approach of generating new programs. Management cannot close its eyes and avoid new programs. But, although these sources are a necessity in law enforcement, reliance on this one avenue through which to induce change can have disastrous overtones. Any sporadic program instruction must be blended into an overall conscious plan. In the absence of such a plan, police organizations are again **reacting** to change, not effectively advancing measurable change. This reactionary type of response perpetuates the knee-jerk approach to management which has so painfully retarded police organizational progress.

When studying this map, police managers need to keep the preceding legend in mind. Questions will arise about each topic on the map. How will the concept, approach, or program fit into the overall advancement of not only a manager's own police agency, but into the advancement of law enforcement as a profession with the future in mind?

Planners should also remember that whether or not you agree with the forecasts, we are all headed for the future. What condition police organizations are in when the **future** is here depends a great deal on what police managers in the 1990s accomplish. Face it. The future is now; it can be influenced.

A MORE PRODUCTIVE DETECTIVE

Contrary to their popular image, detectives are not masters of deduction foiling the plots of incredibly clever criminals by piecing together tiny elements of evidence and circumstances into an arcane, but logical sequence. Neither are they pigheaded stooges bungling all the cases that the private eyes will have to solve. The world of the detective does not glitter. Drug busts are rarely made in million dollar penthouses. There are few diplomats operating houses of prostitution and slave trading posts from the back doors of exquisitely decorated embassies. Heiresses who bump off their favorite dress designer for a one-of-a-kind party dress are scarce these days.... [2]

Images and Myths

The mystique surrounding detective work has been the cause of much of the lack of progress made in criminal investigative efforts. Police service itself perpetuates this mystique by failing to produce well-evaluated procedures for determining the exact role detectives are to play in the missions of their departments. The popular image of detectives, as projected in films, television, and novels, has further damaged the ability of the police organization to accurately define the detective's exact role. Actual investigative work has little, if any, resemblance to the public's image. The truth of the matter is that much of what is resolved by detectives is accomplished because a witness was able to provide a license number, or a suspect left some clue at the crime scene, or, most importantly, the suspect bragged to someone of involvement in the crime. Inductive reasoning plays a limited role and always has. Informant contacts are probably the most important asset an investigator may possess. Detectives are necessary to the everyday operation of a police organization. The question that should be asked arises from the inability of a police organization to identify exactly how much time detectives put in on their jobs with respect to their overall contributions to the organization's mission. The tradition of a uniform officer taking a report, then forwarding the report on to the detective for follow-up, should be challenged for a variety of reasons. The types of crimes traditionally assigned to detectives for follow-up also need to be examined. A greater degree of freedom is automatically awarded to the detective. The detective is usually not assigned to handle dispatches. Although a report writer, he or she is rarely a report taker. What do they do with their time?

There are many hard-working and productive detectives in police service, and what follows is not intended to demean their performance. What follows is just the simple truth about detective work and no-nonsense perspectives upon which police managers should appraise and address roles of detectives in conjunction with the role of police service in the 1990s.

Work Loads

Most police agencies have divided their detectives' assignments according to specialties ranging from the traditionally acclaimed homicide detective to investigations of thefts, robberies, sex crimes, drugs, and vice. Agencies too small to specialize may have detectives assigned to work all of the specialized areas. Debate continues as to the effectiveness of investigators who become too specialized. Agencies which place emphasis on the monthly clearance rates of Part One crimes usually find that they cannot do without the specialization of their detective forces. Less specialization may lead to lower clearance rates, thus causing an organization to face questions about its ability to solve crimes. Whether or not a detective can solve crimes actually loses its true meaning when police organizations rely so heavily upon clearance rates to measure performance. The Rand Corporation report in 1974 first confirmed one of the worst fears of detective commanders across the country. The report, while highly critical of the use of detectives, did support contentions that detectives could be used effectively if their performance gauge was properly set. The Rand Corporation's study serves as a formal back-up to the position of many modern day police managers involved in criminal investigation assignments. The problem may be reduced to a simple mathematical equation which defines the scenario completely.

On the average, a mid-sized police agency serving a population of 200,000 will receive around 30,000 criminal complaints a year. Of these complaints, around 13,200 will be Part One crimes. Most mid-sized agencies have about 15 percent of their total manpower assigned to detective functions. Generally, there are around 50 detectives in a mid-sized department. Now, even though many of these 50 detectives may be assigned to areas like vice or drug enforcement which do not handle Part

One crimes, they will still be factored into the equation in order to demonstrate the fallacies of the existing approach.

Simple division of 50 detectives into 30,000 reported crimes reveals that each detective would be responsible for the investigation of 600 crimes per year, or 50 a month. Now let's reduce the number of detectives to a more realistic figure. Subtract 20 from the original 50 detectives. These 20 will represent those who are assigned to investigate crimes not reflected on Part One crime reports, those who are assigned to vice, narcotics, economic crimes, and administration support assignments critical to detective work. Simple division now makes cases assigned to Part One crimes more unrealistic. Now a detective will be assigned 1,500 cases a year, or 125 cases a month. Once court time, time off, and other assignments are figured into the equation, managers can easily translate the problems and identify the shortcomings of this system. It is impractical and unreasonable to expect any detective to produce outstanding and consistent performance when assigned such an unrealistic number of cases. Although this formula is far from being one that can be used for every police organization and there are going to be fluctuating factors which play into the final figures, we must look at the practical side of this reasoning. Obviously, every single criminal complaint is not assigned to a detective for follow-up.

Solvability Factors

How can a police organization make its detectives more effective in the face of overwhelming numbers of Part One crimes without sacrificing service to the community? In reality, there is no best solution; but, as in all decision-making processes, there are alternatives which can make detectives more effective while still serving the community's interest. Problems which will be encountered are politics and making tough decisions which admit that police service cannot keep up with the workload under present structures. External political forces may demand that the police handle each and every criminal complaint so that it appears the community is receiving full attention on all reported crimes. That concept may continue, and that appearance may be promoted, but it will be a false claim which lessens the credibility of not only the police agency, but the political forces imposing such restrictions.

Increasing the size of the detective force is not the solution either. Remember that early police organizations and politicians responded to all crime problems in the early part of this century by adding manpower, and the additions did nothing to affect the crime rate. An alternative that does provide a solution for the 1990s is one that allows police organizations to work smarter, using the same number of detectives, but to investigate only those reported crimes which the Rand Study identifies as having **solvability factors.** The concept is not new, but the widespread use of the solvability factors would be unique and would further advance all police agencies' investigative responses and crime clearances. Any manager who has served as a detective knows that cases are solved on the basis of available evidence or information. Inductive reasoning plays a role, but the role is limited by the initiative, imagination, and experience of the detective. All detectives do not possess the immediate imagination, experience, and initiative required to effectively exercise inductive reasoning skills, but police organizations can outline a process through which detectives may evaluate criminal reports to determine if the report should be investigated or filed pending further information.

Practically all criminal complaints may be initially evaluated through six principles that have commonly become accepted as solvability factors. Those principles are:

1. Is there a witness to the crime?
2. Is there traceable property?
3. Is there physical evidence which can identify a suspect?
4. Is there a significant method of operation by suspects which can lead to the identification of suspects?
5. Is there reason to believe that public interest aroused by the crime could lead to public assistance which would lead to the solution?
6. Can the suspect be identified by a witness?

When reviewing criminal complaints, a detective may find no solvability factors associated with the crime. If none exist, then the crime should be filed pending further information. Obviously, this type of solvability assessment cannot be used on certain crimes which shock the sensibilities of a community. Murders, serious assaults, major robberies, sex crimes, and major thefts must be investigated regardless of solvability factors. However, the stringent use of the solvability factors to reduce the number of overall assignments to detectives can ultimately improve investigative responses. The approach is based upon a thorough reporting by the uniform officer. Before an agency can undertake this assessment process, managers must assure that their line reporting is competent and thorough enough for an assessor to make a call on the solvability factors. Having the factors listed on the report form and checked by the reporting officer could benefit this process.

Case Assignment Management

Usually, the first objection to a strict use of solvability factors originates from police administrators who must respond not only to the public, but to the external political forces. The concern that there will be additional complaints from the citizenry about the lack of attention from the police on reported crimes should be expected. To minimize initial criticism, managers should plan a letter or mailing card program for all complaints which are not assigned to detectives for follow-up investigations. A standard letter or mailing card, preprinted but not presigned, should be mailed to each complainant that will not have personal contact with a detective. The card or letter will serve to assure the complainant that the report has been reviewed and has received personal attention from the police even though circumstances do not warrant an immediate, active follow-up. The card or letter should be personally signed by a designee who reviewed the complaints or by detective commanders who are assigned the responsibility of case coordination. A letter or card which contains a name and report number goes a long way in promoting the tone necessary in a community for the successful use of solvability factor programs. A sample of what a letter or card should contain would be:

Dear _____:

The report that you recently filed with the (name of police agency) has been reviewed by Criminal Investigation Section personnel. At this point, your case has been placed in an **Open by Active** status. Your case has been assigned a report number, _____, to which you can refer in the future, should you learn additional facts. If you wish to inquire about your case, please call Monday through Friday, 8 a.m. to 5 p.m., and ask for _____.

Your case is one of many received by the Criminal Investigation Section. Each case is important, and we will give your case as much consideration as possible. Please be advised that certain things will be done in each case, but that you will not be personally contacted by the Criminal Investigation Section unless we need further information or we have solved your case.

Investigation includes:

• All serial-numbered items will be entered into the national and state-wide computer.

- Teletypes will be sent out to other agencies where the items stolen or the suspect, if known, can be identified.
- Local pawn records will be checked daily.
- Fingerprints of known criminals using the same methods that were used in your case will be checked.
- Arrests of criminals made by the Division of Police will be closely checked to see if they could be responsible for your offense. Their fingerprints will be checked, where applicable.
- Property held by this department or other departments will be closely checked in an effort to return it to the legal owner.

You have a responsibility to:

- Make every effort to obtain any serial numbers of articles stolen.
- Keep the investigative officer advised of any information you may learn that will be of assistance to the investigation.
- Make sure that you list all stolen items in your report as accurately as possible, so that officers of this agency or any other agency receiving our teletype will have the best possible description of your property.
- If the return of your property or prosecution of the offender(s) is important to you, you must keep your police department notified of any change of address you may make. We cannot return your property or prosecute any offender without you.

Other points to consider:

- Take measures to make yourself, your house, apartment, or store more secure against future attacks or intruders. Consider marking your valuable items with your drivers license number, social security number, or other suitable number for positive identification if stolen.
- Record serial numbers of items and keep them in a safe place.
- Place valuable items, such as jewelry, in a safe deposit box.

Keep in mind that your police department will make every effort to locate your property and/or arrest the offender, but officers must rely on you to supply the most accurate and up-to-date information available.

Sincerely,

—————————————————————
Criminal Investigation Section

The costs associated with mailings should not overly concern managers. The time and costs saved by detectives not being required to handle cases which have no solvability factors should offset any mailing costs. The benefits of public contacts from these mailings is intangible, but should be considered as a bonus when considering cost concerns.

Managers should also consider the studies conducted in the 1970s based upon the Rand Corporation's findings. These examples, although almost twenty years old, still serve as a foundation to further streamline the work of the detective before the increase in demands that will be made in the 1990s. Studies in which a strict adherence to the solvability principles were used show that clearances increase along with the community's confidence in the police. Allocation of investigative resources to only those cases which have a true probability of solution makes good sense. External political factors and the community itself cannot expect police organizations to continue traditionally unproductive investigative approaches which diminish the overall effectiveness of their police department. This is one area which must be explained thoroughly to the public; but, once explained, it is doubtful if any external influence will demand a return to the old, self-defeating process.

POLICE AND THE MEDIA: CONFLICTS, INFLUENCE, AND DIALOGUE

In the 1970s, police cultures paid attention to the power of the media. Perhaps it was the savage reviews of police service by the media in the 1960s that sharpened administrators' awareness of the post-Watergate years which focused on the contention that America's free media had proven itself to be as important as the designers of the Constitution had meant it to be. Police-media relations training was developed during this period, and a vastly improved police-media relationship was beginning to develop. Although the interdependency between the media and police was only tokenly acknowledged in the 1970s, both coexist more effectively in times of crisis, a reflection of their mutual interest. As the 1980s pass, the police-media relationship has finally been placed in a perspective more conducive to the development of the **partnership** necessary to most benefit society.

The most common complaint from journalists and police stems from the allegation that neither group knows nearly enough about the working world of the other.[3] Planners familiar with historical roots of how the media began its original crime coverage when the police organization was first getting started may hold better insight into how the relationship began and why it led to differences. From that perspective, a planner may be able to quickly grasp the necessity of interdependency for the future.

The Evolution of the Relationship

The London Metropolitan Police, established in 1929 [through British Home Secretary, Sir Robert Peel's Metropolitan Police Act], is widely accepted as the first **organized police agency** in the western world. The social disorder rampant in England at the time brought acceptance to Peel's concept which centralized all of the various independent police forces working in London. The marine police, merchant police, Bow Street Runners, Parish Police, and many unsanctioned vigilante groups were disbanded, and the Metropolitan Police became the single, unified police force for that city. Eventually, this police agency was to be headquartered in the former residence of the Kings of Scotland. The large building had an open courtyard through which the building was entered, thus the headquarters of this **new** police organization became known as **Scotland Yard**.[4]

Peel was placed in charge of the new operation, and suddenly the press was faced with its first centralized release of crime information to the public from an organization holding all the information. This approach was far from what the press had been used to in their daily dealings with the various **quasi-police** groups which had agreeably allowed the press access to any existing record, crime scene, or other information. While Peel's organization did not hamper the efforts of reporters to gather crime information, they were suddenly cast as the only resource for **behind the scenes** information.

In the 1820s, the press had discovered that if presented harshly, the news of crime and violence had mass appeal. Charles Dickens was a police reporter during this period in England, and his writings not only covered this type of reporting, but of the courts and their abuses.[5] The British tabloids of the period were filled with accounts of brutal crimes and often portrayed Peel and his **Bobbies** as heroes of sorts, but the appeal of sensationally reported violence gradually became disrupted by Peel's organization. Less and less information was made available to the press over the first 10 years of their existence. This slow strangulation, often a result of the organization's attempt to prevent damaging leaks about internal problems as well as to limit unnecessary details about particularly violent crime, soon led to another type of relationship with an ever-inquiring press.

What started out as a blissful relationship, at least for that period in British society, turned into a suspicion-based courtship which made police feel that the press was deficient in reporting about their better qualities. Unsurprisingly, the press felt that the police were not only uncooperative, but perhaps concealing. These views led to **press policies** being established, creating the inevitable butting of heads which set the tone for police-media relationships for decades to come.

The development of municipal policing in America took much the same course, but America was mostly rural at the time and there were only a few cities that had populations sufficient to assure wide readership of the daily crime and violence news. Regardless, a similar tone and relationship soon emerged between American police and press. An expanding and new democratic country offered much more to hold the reader's interests than did crime and violence. In the 1920s, crime news seldom occupied more than 5 percent of the total news space in the various newspapers across the country.[6] The social phenomenon of the press can be easily exampled from a 1928 study of 100 newspapers in America. The study covered a 75-year time span and revealed that crime coverage averaged less than 1.4 percent of the total editorial material. Polls at the time revealed that most people thought the coverage would be as high as 50 percent.[7] This study may accurately pinpoint the true power of the press, suggesting that small amounts of crime coverage energize large crime-wave impressions.[8]

Print Media and Broadcast Journalism

With this example in mind, planners should be capable of appreciating the extent of impact of the printed media, but newspapers are just one of journalism's powerful impression-makers today. Planners must still learn to understand and appreciate one of the greatest social influences of the 20th century: television.[9]

In the late 1940s and early 1950s, television's singular purpose was entertainment. Politics changed that, and the reverberations from the Eisenhower-Stevenson presidential campaign in 1952 paved the way for television news to be recognized as a potentially formidable competitor to radio and the printed news. Polls in the 1980s claim that the American public receives about 75 percent of their news from television, and the emergence of national networks concentrating on nothing but the headline and world news, 24 hours a day, seems to collaborate the nation's hunger for immediate coverage of daily events.

This type of broadcast journalism has evolved into a highly emotional and immediate impression-making form of news reporting. It shows all sides of brutal and tragic incidents, sometimes as it's happening. Its affects can be seen in the attitudes and by the rejection or acceptance by society of a variety of cultural transformations ranging from the images cast of the flower generation to the nightly horror shown on the evening news of the Vietnam War. Its up-to-the-minute reporting ability has been widely credited with making the news, such as the resignation of an American President and the fluctuation of the New York Stock Exchange. Without question, the broadcasts of the 1960s, which vividly displayed the performance of police across the country in dealing with social disruption, led to massive police reform movements.

While newspapers and radio news may lay claim to some of the same credit, they cannot match the **headline news** impact of television's imagery capabilities. The major advantage of newspapers over television journalism is that their stories contain more detail. Press reporters can take more time to become familiar with the story line than can their competitors who are scurrying to meet the deadline for an evening broadcast. Often that time is what makes a story more accurate. The press reporter is under less space and time constraints to tell the story. A broadcast journalist may have less than a minute to pack in all the details of a headline story, whereas the newspaper reporter may have half of the entire front page. The more details making up the story are frequently found to be the formula which makes the reporting more accurate and balanced. Considering the opinion-setting capabilities of the media, newspapers are by far the most suitable format through which organizations may expect a completely balanced view.

Investigative Reporting

Another brand of journalist style surfaced in the 1970s, which further stiffened police postures toward the media. Television has its share of investigative journalism, but newspapers are able to utilize their staffs much more effectively. The pursuit of investigative journalism with Watergate-inspired zeal has made it often appear that newspapers have lost interest in the more mundane crimes like armed robbery or burglary. The **investigative reporter** now tracks stories which have a **corruption angle,** or one that is interpreted as an exposé. This is the stuff of which Pulitzer Prizes are made, and this new breed of reporter will pursue such stories relentlessly.[10] Investigative reporters, while basically performing the same job as police officers—reporting facts—are still often seen by officers as amateurs, wildly reporting information based on anonymous sources with unbridled speculation as their guidance system. This view is true in many cases of newspaper and television **investigative reporting,** but planners must admit that law enforcement is often fertile ground for this type of journalism, and both institutions will suffer from amateurish actions in defense and response. There will always be **unbridled speculations,** but strong and well-founded interrelationships between all levels of police and the media will go a long way in predefining the difference between reporting the facts and giving rise to this type of journalistic endeavor. It remains unfortunate that lesser control exists for exercise by either institution over the individual quirks and personality conflicts between individual officers and reporters.

Many journalists, editors, and students of journalism will argue the purpose of the press in America. Regardless of what anyone claims, the press is a business. It is not exactly the same commercial-type venture of other businesses, but there are consumer sales and profits to be examined along with the principles of professional journalism. Arguments will inevitably follow when police discuss the First Amendment with the press. Are reporters actually surrogates of the public? Do they protect the public? Does the Bill of Rights actually appoint them as protectors? It all comes down to how the Constitution is interpreted, and often this attitude toward the press by police agencies is simply unnecessary.

Police Response Integrity

The First Amendment will continue to guarantee free speech, and police organizations may be assured that they will be held accountable for their actions whether they like it or not. There is no sense in a police organization failing to respond to the legitimate inquiries of the media. How an agency responds sets the tone for the relationship between the media and police. The media may not particularly like or agree with a police agency's response on a variety of issues; but, if the response is fair, accurate, and available, and if the agency is consistent in its response policy, the media is likely to become an asset for police service. Under these conditions, the media will more quickly understand and accept the limits on a police organization's release of information. Contrary to what has often been popular consensus within police circles, it is not up to the media to develop a close working relationship with the police.

Police officers negotiate with people as part of their daily work. They provide direction, relay orders, and question people on issues that will directly affect other peoples' lives. Police managers communicate on a multitude of topics that directly affect critical issues of the entire organization, yet it is staggering to see how many police officers and police managers freeze when approached by a reporter. An officer may make a statement to a suspect in an investigation upon which an appeal is based, and the officer's name ends up forever emblazoned in the annals of case law precedents in the American court system . . . sometimes unfavorably. Many shrug off encounters or refuse comments based on the assumption that they will automatically be misquoted or made to look like a fool on the evening news. Others desperately attempt to present themselves as having all the facts when, in the final analysis, they wind up saying nothing about what they were asked. Some ease through the encounter, choosing their words carefully, and simply talk like a person, not just as a police officer. There is no perfect way to be interviewed. There are too many variables that play into any situation to use the same standard responses or tight-jawed appearance. People will be misquoted. Not everyone looks good on television and, yes, mistakes will happen. Police must accept that the media will always be inquiring. That is the nature of the business. How police respond will assuredly dictate the type of relationship an agency will have with the media in any community. The effectiveness of certain aspects of crime control programs and community involvement in the 1990s may depend upon the ability of police managers to deal with the media. Police managers who learn the key ingredients of **response integrity** and who put those ingredients to work at every opportunity when dealing with members of the media will immediately enhance their agency's effectiveness.

Police Response Policies

Police managers and administrators have to face some facts if they are to begin to be successful in their dealings with the media. Modern police leaders, especially those who are in executive level positions, are public figures; it is unreasonable to think that they will not have to deal with being the focus of the media.[11] Planners must concentrate on what can be done by them and their agencies in order to utilize the media's assets to the benefit of the organization and to minimize potential harm. The most potentially harmful aspect which must be considered stems from the reasons police organizations do what they do. Are they valid? The police-media conflicts which traditionally exist can be modified tremendously if a policy is in place addressing their coexistence and preventing either group from feeling put upon.[12]

Police departments often assume the attitudes of their leaders with respect to their feelings about the media in general. The feeling that the media is **out to get the police** primarily comes from the actions of the leaders. While officers may have some of those concerns to start with, their feelings are **confirmed** once a police chief or other leaders in the organization start to make negative comments about the media. This sets the tone, and the entire organization may be affected.[13]

To a certain degree, police and the media have some things in common. Both speak highly of their importance to the community; both are powerful, visible institutions; both are secretive about their methods of operation and frequently rely upon anonymous sources for information; and, when it comes to criticism, neither appears especially adept at acknowledging its own failing.[14]

Attitudinal changes based upon a finely tuned interrelationship will thaw the **cold war** between the two, but that defrosting should be expedited in order for a police service to be more effective in its community, especially in the 1990s.

Knowing the Local Media

Police managers need to be more aware of local media. Even managers who rarely deal with the media should have some background on what their agency must do in order to fully cooperate with the legitimate inquiries from television, radio, and newspapers. Most departmental general orders contain a policy on **handling the media.** Often these policies address how the agency responds to inquiries, who may respond, what information may be released, and how to handle the media at crime scenes. The fundamentals are there, but a vast amount of practical information is often absent, inadvertently feeding the ongoing but unwritten opposition most police organizations extend to the media. More details are necessary in these departmental orders and guidelines; but, in the meantime, more overtures from the police are necessary, as well as changes in the way police think about the media.

Public Information Officers

Many large and mid-sized police organizations have found that the use of a public information officer (PIO) has enhanced their working relationship with the media. The PIO concept was borne from the necessity of centralizing the information released from an organization. Some departments designate one or more officers to be the spokesman for the agency on all matters of public concern. All news releases, announcements, and inquiries are handled by or channeled through the PIO. The FBI uses the PIO concept most effectively. One or two agents in an office are designated to these positions and are the only agents authorized to be interviewed by the media or to release information about FBI actions other than a recognized supervisor. The FBI uses this concept not only to control outgoing information, but to assure that a trained spokesman represents the Bureau and that the media has an authorized source from which to solicit information. The FBI's use of this concept makes it a very sterile form of media cooperation, but it is highly effective for that agency. Members of the media rely heavily upon the PIO in the Bureau, but most agree that much of the information released appears processed.

However, the FBI is not a community-oriented law enforcement agency. They do not represent the vast cross sections of people in various communities; therefore, they are not expected or required to respond to the media in the same manner as expected from a local or state police agency. Those agencies are comprised of people who are a visible part of the community. While a high standard of responsiveness to the public, through the media, is expected from local and state police, communities should also witness and be able to relate to the involvement of the organization in local activities without the sterility associated with a PIO program.

The 1990s will require more of a humanistic response from police service in matters of **handling the media**. The PIO program can work well, but managers must be aware of the need to ensure that an agency does not appear to be less involved with the community because there is only one or two spokesmen or that information appears automated and manufactured to fit the situation. PIO programs are sometimes seen as barriers by the media. Even though most PIO concepts are based on the principle that any officer may talk with the media, many officers and managers choose to use the program as a means to justify avoiding the media. This does little to further advance community familiarization with the officers and leaders.

Some agencies still rely on the traditional approach of permitting only supervisors and commanders to respond to media inquiries. Although closer to the style necessary to broaden a community's view of their police department, this approach still lacks a degree of humanism necessary for the 1990s.

PIO programs or policies which dictate that supervisors and commanders are primarily responsible for media inquiries prevent the fundamental encouragement needed for police officers to become a visible working part of the community. A PIO program can lead to internal disgruntlement where viewed by some officers as being designed to allow only the PIO to represent their agency. A PIO's demeanor, appearance, and professional ability will go a long way; but, if the PIO has little credibility among the ranks, internal conflicts will arise. It makes little difference whether a PIO is a ranking officer or a patrolman, as long as the PIO has command of the knowledge required to intelligently represent the agency. The only people who will ever fully recognize the credibility of the PIO are the officers within an agency. They will know the PIO's background, experience, and true credentials. The internal support of PIO-styled programs rests with management's selection of the internally credible PIOs.

Expanding the Relationships

A greater bond will be required between the media and police in the 1990s as police service becomes more and more community-oriented. Community involvement will automatically open police organizations up to more media scrutiny. Police agencies will continue to rely upon rigid guidelines through which to handle specific inquiries from the media. These regulations will not diminish, and legal decisions in the future will most likely impose additional restraints on what police officers may or may not say about criminally-related matters. This area of media relations must be distinguished from the other areas that police must enhance with the media, particularly marketing community-oriented concepts.

Most police officers and managers attempt to cooperate with reporters with whom they frequently deal. Regardless of departmental procedures, the one-on-one relationships that are often forged between police and reporters arise from a base of mutual respect and understanding that stems from dealing with each other in an honest and open manner. Any reporter worth his salt will have at least one contact in a police agency from whom information may always be obtained. Any police manager worth his salt is also going to have a reporter from whom the same courtesies apply. Managers should be encouraging police-media contacts as often as possible. Let the media into closed circles as much as possible; let them see the mistakes along with the actions that most police agencies would like to see touted. Humanize the relationship. This approach helps offset the negatives as well as the sometimes erroneous contention that the police and the media were meant to always disagree. Managers may not feel comfortable in encouraging the humanizing approach to police-media relations, but managers will have to agree that the media is needed by the police service in the future. The media will be the only viable and dependable resource capable of widespread distribution of information which is becoming so critical to police agencies through community-oriented policing.

Informal Police-Media Meetings

In recent years, police-media meetings have served a useful purpose. The meetings, which usually take place once every two or three months, are hosted by one of the participating organizations at a time most convenient to participants. In addition to the broadcast and print media reporters being invited to these meetings, editors and news directors are encouraged to attend, as are higher echelon administrators. Other agencies, such as fire departments, civil defense representatives, and armed forces representatives, are sometimes included. Informal meetings allow off-the-record discussions of recent incidents relative to criminal justice, public safety, and the media, and offer a platform through which differences in opinion or working policies may be ironed out between the participants.

This approach breaks down barriers rapidly by exposing strengths and weaknesses in each participant's field. Often new approaches to handling old problems arise from informal discussion and group involvement on a problem. Responsibility to organize the meetings should be undertaken by one of the police agencies involved. A police manager should identify the media representatives, present a brief outline addressing the purpose of the meetings, frequency of the meetings, and the off-the-record status of the meetings. The initiator should host the first meeting and accept the responsibility of chairing the sessions unless other agencies or media participants are willing to take the time and effort to plan the session on a regular basis. At the first meeting, the following representatives should be invited:

1. Editors of all local newspapers and news directors for local television and radio stations.
2. Reporters most frequently covering criminal justice stories from radio, television, and print media in the area.
3. Local police chiefs, assistant chiefs, PIOs, and/or those police personnel most frequently involved with responding to media inquiries.
4. Heads of other public safety agencies/organizations.

Once ground rules are established, announcements should be made within the police organization outlining the purpose and frequency of the meetings. From this point on, police managers should be encouraging personnel from all ranks and assignments to attend the meetings and openly discuss their views, as well as current problems dealing with media inquiries and relationships. The same encouragement should be given to the members of the media to return to their organizations and encourage attendance from all levels.

One shortcoming of this approach usually surfaces after completion of a couple of meetings. Higher echelon representatives from all agencies often relinquish their involvement, thus leaving only those who are not in the position of setting or changing agency policy or procedures. While many benefits remain when only the reporters and middle-level or line-level police participate, the purpose of the meetings generally suffer when there are no policy-makers present. Many of the changes that come from meetings address the day-to-day needs of reporters in obtaining accurate information from the police agency, as well as minor adjustments in the way police may make their responses more efficient without sacrificing the major principles behind policy. The biggest benefit to all participants comes from sitting in on an informal meeting where differences may be exposed, circumstances discussed, and ideas exchanged between the people who have distinctly separate goals and functions.

The frequency and locations of the meetings should be arranged to accommodate the attendance of necessary participants and, importantly, the police should be initiator of this program. An ingenuous effort must be put forth by the police to include the media in the organization's plans for the future. These meetings can offset problems which must be dealt with sooner or later as the police organization changes with the community. Programs which involve the media almost to the extent of making them a full-time partner will generate the humanizing concept which is necessary for the 1990s. Enlisting the media in this and other programs not only introduces them to a side of criminal justice they have rarely been able to witness firsthand, but it provides the public with another perspective on the relationship between the media and police. This **working together** perspective adds the credibility to police organizations and further erodes the stereotypical images the public has of the media and police. These images also dissolve negative perceptions by the police of the media, and by the media of the police.

Ordinarily, police and the media have not made ideal partners in crime solving. That has changed through one of the most revolutionary crime solving programs of this century. The program has not only blended the wide exposure offered through the media for the police to request help from the communities in crime solving, it has introduced the media into community-oriented policing by making the public see both entities as partners in making their community safer. The next stop on this road map provides details.

COMMUNITY INVOLVEMENT IN CRIME SOLVING—
CRIME STOPPERS

In 1976, Albuquerque, New Mexico, initiated a program which was destined to evolve into one of the fastest growing crime solving programs in the United States. Called Crime Stoppers, the program was founded upon the recognition that citizen cooperation is an essential and crucial element in solving crimes. The program offered a way to open investigative doors that were otherwise closed. A more participative crime-solving tone is established through the program and, most importantly, the program provides a means for the public to feel like they are doing something tangible in fighting crime.

Unlike other programs introduced by the police over the past decades, Crime Stoppers is self-sustaining; the burden of costs, manpower, and implementation does not fall on the shoulders of the police agency. A new alliance surfaces through Crime Stoppers, one that must be accepted as the future norm.

A decade of research shows that Crime Stopper programs, also known as Crime Solvers, Crime Line, Secret Witness, or other titles, is not a panacea nor will it substantially cause a reduction in the overall crime rate. A small percentage of the total serious crimes in a community will be resolved through the program, but the overall impact and no-nonsense application of the program will do more to develop support for police agencies than a temporary increase in the clearance of serious crimes during a brief reporting period.

The program places the community, media, and law enforcement in concert. A nonprofit corporation, once established, sets the program's policy, raises funds, and coordinates the cash reward system through a board of directors comprised of community leaders who will dedicate time to the marketing of the program and fund raising. Usually, the length of time a board member sits is established by a predetermined period of appointment. Appointments are made by invitation or through request, and seats on the board are filled as appointments expire. Usually, no police officials sit on the board.

The Role of the Media

The media educates the public about the program, funds are raised by the board from private businesses, and the police department staffs and houses the program. Local television stations become involved by broadcasting a reenactment of a crime on a weekly basis. The **Crime of the Week** is produced by a broadcast media participant. The information upon which to produce the TV broadcast is obtained by the police coordinators. Often those officers are made a part of the broadcast through short interviews. The reenactment is commonly done through the use of police officers or local volunteers to agree to act the parts. In the end, the public will see how the crime was committed on television, a reward is offered for information leading to the arrest of persons responsible for committing the crime, and the public is provided with the program's telephone number. An important point reminds the public that callers remain anonymous.

Some programs only use the print media or radio stations to announce the particulars of the **Crime of the Week,** and this approach works well but not as effectively as the recreation on television. Often a television station will broadcast the reenactment during regular news casts. The short recreation may also prove effective when shown at other times of the day. Newspapers usually run the program's advertisement about the

Crime of the Week once a week, preferably on the same day as the broadcast.

In addition to the **Crime of the Week,** programs may also develop a fugitive or wanted list to occasionally air or to be printed. This approach identifies persons, most often through photographs, who are wanted by police for various crimes, and a reward is offered for their apprehension.

Some agencies that would like to develop the reenactment approach often throw up their hands in frustration, because they are unable to access a major television station. A joint program made up of several counties could resolve this problem. Instead of creating a program that will only assist one community, planners should consider a program that will assist several communities at one time. After all, criminal activity does not automatically stop at the county line. A major benefit in this concept is that regional programs widen the base of fund raising. They also further the realization that all of us are in this thing together, and communities should unite in responding to crime control issues.

Under this regional concept, one law enforcement agency should assume responsibility for coordination between the other communities and other police agencies. Calls should still come into one central telephone number so that record-keeping may remain accurate. This is particularly important when rewards are to be paid later.

If a program is to be designed using television reenactments, and those reenactments will be seen by people in several communities, each of those communities should be encouraged to participate in the development of the program.

When planning a program, one of the first questions to be addressed is cost. Personnel costs are easily determined by the number of people an agency needs to assign as full-time program coordinators. The number of officers will be determined by the size of the program, communities, and police agencies involved.

Program Organization for Success

When considering costs, remember that the program is designed to address those crimes that are unlikely to be resolved through routine police services and those cases which remain unresolved regardless of law enforcement resources or the amount of time put into the investigation.

Crime Stoppers International recently reported that in one year, all of the programs in the United States were accredited with solving 92,339 felony crimes. An average of $6,089 worth of stolen property was recovered per case, and rewards totaled $6,728,392.[15] The program's success is usually attributed to the use of rewards, but a Lake County, Illinois, study showed that the reward size had virtually no affect on the caller's motive to participate.

In Lexington, Kentucky, a regional Crime Stoppers program developed in 1987 covers seven counties with television, radio, and print media participation. The program reenacted 52 crimes in 12 months. Of these crimes, six were solved and a total of $12,775 was paid in rewards. Amazingly, 20 percent of the callers refused the reward being offered. Reaching almost 400,000 people, this program resolved two five-year-old homicide investigations during its first three months of operation.

Although Crime Stoppers programs motivate callers through rewards and the guarantee of anonymity, the ultimate success of the program still rests with the police who investigate the tips. Program personnel are best utilized as coordinators and investigators. Tips are usually documented and forwarded to the unit or squad which originally investigated the offense. The result of the follow-up investigation is reported back to the program coordinators for reference and record-keeping, as well as for reward payment considerations.

The board of directors decides the amount of rewards paid to callers based upon recommendations of the coordinators. Set rewards for the **Crime of the Week** do not vary, but rewards for certain information relayed to the program that lead to an arrest or property recovery may be paid. Payments are controlled through the use of code numbers assigned callers by the coordinator.

Obviously, competent program coordinators are a requisite for the agency planning a program. Failing to select the right people for this assignment immediately limits the program's potential for success. Coordinators must work effectively with the public, local businesses, and investigators; they must participate in the reenactments, and they must perform the follow-up coordination.

It is extremely important that the program coordinators screen the information they receive from the program. Investigators who are flooded with every bit of information received may start questioning the usefulness of the program. Equally important is the balance that coordinators must establish in this screening process. Too much screening may result in the coordinators taking on the role of investigator. This, too, can undermine the purpose of the program.

Planners should look at other agencies on how their programs have been integrated into their organizations. Placement of the program in community services, or the traditional crime prevention bureau, tends to limit success. Assigning the program as part of the agency's criminal investigation section seems to work best. After all, coordinators must coordinate; not just with the media and the callers, but also with the people responsible for following up the leads.

Some legal issues are often brought up about the Crime Stoppers programs. With only a little over a decade of experience, there are no pat answers to all questions. There are concerns about protecting civilian board members from liability for false arrest. Other concerns stem from questions about upholding the anonymity of callers.

Incorporation of the program is one solution; carrying claim insurance another. Basic research by planners into how existing programs best fit both community and agency needs will provide most of these answers.

Planners should not expect too many immediate changes in community attitudes about the program, particularly not in a short period of time. Some factors of police service are still reserved about the concept. The relatively new strategy is just that ... a new strategy. It works very well in many of the over 600 programs throughout the United States. It is a positive and certainly productive way to help solve crimes.

The question a planner must answer is whether or not the benefits of the program outweigh the benefits of methods currently used. If the answer is yes, planners know their next step: Research.

DRUG ENFORCEMENT AND EDUCATION STRATEGIES

In 1914, the United States began regulating the use of drugs through the Harrison Act. This legislation set a tone which has led the nation to believe that the sale, use, and distribution of a controlled substance is a singular crime, that police can deal with violators, and that government can effectively regulate drugs by enforcement legislation. It was not until the 1980s that police managers began to seriously question the wisdom of this unwritten strategy and began to show concern about the link between drugs and all crimes. Police efforts to control drug distribution have been essentially futile for the past five decades. The police response to rising drug problems in the mid-sixties was to seek more funding, increase the size of drug enforcement functions, and arrest users and traffickers in the belief that drugs should not be used simply because they are **against the law.**

As with other program failures, police planning was not in synchronization with the causes behind the explosion in drug usage. Most police agencies stumbled forward in their unavailing attempts to interdict drugs through strict enforcement. The amounts of money spent on drug enforcement is staggering. In 1988, the Federal government allocated a total of $20.6 billion for Federal, state, and local law enforcement spending; but, surprisingly, this figure represents only around six-tenths of 1 percent of the total federal budget for 1988.[16] Conversely, a United States Customs Service Survey in 1987 revealed that of those state and local police agencies participating in the survey, 18.2 percent of their total resources was spent on enforcement of drug laws. The study states that this percentage of resources translates into around $4.9 billion, an $800 million increase over the preceding year. The study went on to report that state and local drug enforcement efforts represent over three-quarters of the drug enforcement efforts in the entire country. Obviously, an incredible river of funds is being poured into drug enforcement, yet enforcement efforts are assessed as ineffective in thwarting the flow of illicit drugs into this country. More bad news, validated through research, confirms that much of the overall crime rate in this country can and should be attributed to the drug trade. The United States Customs survey suggested that on the average, 20 percent of all murders are drug-related; and 25 percent of all auto thefts, 40 percent of all robberies and assaults, and 50 percent of all burglaries and thefts are a result of the link between drugs and other crimes. Other studies reported those figures much higher and assert that 75 percent of all robberies and 50 percent of all felony assaults are linked to drug availability.[17]

Drug enforcement efforts and strategies practiced over the past 20 years are the epitome of the proverbial **vicious cycle.** Police organizations remain frozen in the belief that more manpower and more money must be dedicated to the problem. The concept is not entirely wrong, but the automatic reaction reflects poor planning. This usually stems from the public and political sentiment against drugs, sentiments based upon emotional reactions. Even now, when most police managers agree that drugs influence other crimes and that drug enforcement alone is not the cure, police organizations still stand firmly behind the contention that more money needs to be dedicated to pure enforcement efforts. Many planners have yet to break out of the mold of their predecessors' beliefs that crime problems are only solved with bigger and bigger budgets. The police are the first component of the criminal justice system to see the influences of drug demands translated into crimes. They are also one of the first, if not the first, components of the system which should be researching and recommending new avenues that will lessen the demand for drugs in their respective communities. But the expansion of Federal allocations continues, and police organizations learned long ago how to offset modest state and local appropriations with help from Washington.

The nation is experiencing revitalized concern about drug availability as this decade comes to a close. Election years and recent media exposure given to the risk of crack cocaine in the drug market has helped heighten awareness of America's drug problems. New legislation emphasizing drug-free work places, zero tolerances, mandatory drug testing, and the use of the military in specific drug interdiction work is being formulated. A shift in attention from suppliers to users is being witnessed, and the establishment of a Federal Cabinet level **czar** to coordinate all antidrug activities has become law. This revitalization will cost the nation another $3 billion yearly with **new** programs touching the judiciary, corrections, and treatment programs. State and local police will get their cuts as more 50-50 matching grants become available. The amount being planned for state and local program funding exceeds $1.75 billion, roughly $35 million per state. As usual, funding will be appropriated by population and staggered over a several year period.

An increase in funding will again focus additional attention on drug enforcement efforts. More programs, more seizures, and more arrests will undoubtedly result. Police managers should be leery of the statistics which will surface as a result of these increased strategy efforts. As with any police function, more activity will be generated if more emphasis is assigned to a specific problem. If 10 drug enforcement officers arrest 500 suspects a year, 20 drug enforcement officers will probably arrest 1,000 drug suspects a year. This type of statistical information is often mis-represented and sometimes simply misunderstood by police managers. Doubling an effort will certainly enhance results in terms of enforcement, but those results do not automatically suggest progress or revelations that the problem is actually worse than originally thought (which could arm a planner with data to justify further increases).

Drug enforcement is one of the newest problems to police service, even though drug availability has been a topical issue since the mid-sixties. It has taken most police agencies 15 years to understand

and respond to the drug availability problems with an agency-wide strategy instead of addressing the problems through the traditional one-dimensional **narcotics squad** designed to arrest drug offenders. Although police have just not learned yet how to be truly effective when addressing the problems associated with drug availability, a long-term strategy for drug enforcement is still in the infant stages. Various shifts in loosely planned strategies have caused inevitable stumbling in police approaches to drug enforcement. Police have targeted users, targeted traffickers, targeted manufacturers, formed joint task forces, and used reverse buys on drug dealing suspects in order to make cases against those who are profiting in the trade. Through this maze of strategies, supplies have not been reduced and availability continues to be nurtured because of the demand for drugs created by the past two generations of users making up the bulk of the illicit drug buyers in the United States.

As the 1990s approach, some legislators, government officials, and police contend that some drugs should be legalized in order to take the profit out of the trade, thus reducing the criminal influences associated with illicit drug availability. Dr. Bennette's fourth crimewarp suggests that society's attitudes will ultimately give way to this problem and that there will eventually be a legalization wave across the nation. The forecast and the occasional call for legalization creates further controversy; but whether or not there is a legalization wave in the future depends mostly on the outcome of drug enforcement and police-orchestrated drug education endeavors in the 1990s. Another decade of efforts which fail to curb drug demands will probably do more to cause the public to swing toward legalization theories than anything else. The drug problem may be one area in which police have only one chance to demonstrate that they can effectively carry out the overwhelming mandates of a community to reduce drug availability. If police managers continue to address the problems as they have been addressed over the past two decades, chances are very slim that the 1990s will produce anything more than increasing budgets and vacillation between one unworkable strategy to the next.

Police managers have a wealth of experience to draw upon when planning an effective, long-range drug enforcement policy. Rarely have planners been afforded the luxury of reviewing so many approaches to a problem before selecting their alternatives. It is also rare that police planners immediately have the support of the public on an issue as they do with drug availability concerns. For once, police managers also have at their fingertips access to extravagant sums of funding to address their problems. What may work well for one agency will not always accommodate the needs of another, so managers must use caution in designing a strategy that precisely fits immediate problems, as well as the problems they anticipate facing over the next decade. The map for drug enforcement blends a return to the fundamentals with maximized use of legislative tools and funding made available in the past few years. The map also emphasizes **department wide** strategy planning for ultimate impact and outlines a very simple, workable plan that requires two elements. Without these elements, the blueprints will fail and an agency will continue to stumble through traditional drug enforcement practices. In order for the plan to be successful, there must be: (1) a long-term commitment by managers and administrators to stick to the strategy, and (2) a commitment to involve the police agency in formal drug education and awareness programs to alter attitudes about drug wages and make drug abuse less socially acceptable.

Element A: Nine Enforcement Strategy Principles

Enforcement strategy is founded upon nine principles which round out a police agency's commitment. The principles provide and address the fundamental categories that planners should build upon in order to make the strategy workable for their respective communities. The principles are:

1. meaningful and measurable goals and objectives for the entire agency;
2. designation of a full-time specialized drug enforcement office and its proper staffing;
3. aggressive asset forfeiture policies and accounts to establish and assure perpetual funding of the strategy;
4. encouragement of internal and external reporting of drug offenses accompanied by an organized investigative response;
5. inclusion of all uniform officers in selective drug enforcement patrol techniques;
6. the organized use of drug detection animals;
7. clearly designated responsibilities of investigators assigned to the specialized function;
8. aggressive pursuit of available federal funding; and
9. high public visibility of achievements through proper coordination with the media.

Most police organizations serving a population of 100,000 or more have in place drug enforcement offices which handle all drug enforcement responsibilities. Smaller agencies usually opt to generalize their drug enforcement response which requires that existing detectives handle drug enforcement duties in addition to other assignments. Regardless of the size of a police agency, attention toward the usefulness and effectiveness of a specialized squad, unit, or small group of detectives who handle only drug enforcement is necessary for the 1990s. Even a two-man drug enforcement office in smaller police agencies can efficiently coordinate the strategy outlined in this map. The key is commitment to the program by police managers and administrators, and an understanding of **long-term** planning benefits.

Principle Number 1: Measurable Goals and Objectives. A concise department-wide strategy defines the responsibilities of each officer when drug offenses are suspected or reported, or when arrests are effected. (It is incredulous to set goals through traditional police activity standards such as increased drug arrests. That type of measurement does not establish a means through which progress may be analyzed.) This strategy identifies the most predominantly available drugs in a community, then addresses how the entire agency may work more realistically to reduce illicit supplies. Indicators which are measurable and useful in close examination of a program's progress include such categories as:

- increase and decrease in the types of drug removals (seizures);
- increase and decrease in the reporting of drug offenses from within the agency and from external reporting by the public;
- total agency drug arrests and Part One crime arrests which can be documented as being influenced by drug availability;
- increases and decreases in overdose reports from hospital emergency rooms, and the types of drugs involved;
- monthly listings of the street prices of the various drugs being purchased through controlled buys to identify availability factors (higher prices suggest decreased availability);
- number of street level offenses versus major violator offenses;
- asset forfeitures awarded versus seizures; and
- age and race of defendants arrested for drug offenses.

There are innumerable other categories of activities which will be performed by drug enforcement detectives ranging from surveillances to court time. However, these categories do little to enhance a manager's ability to gauge directions of future problems or to identify areas where more concentration of efforts is necessary. The initial phase of the strategy cannot be evaluated until this type of measurable activity is compiled over several months. A long-term commitment is necessary.

Principle Number 2: Full-Time Attention. Effective drug enforcement must originate from full-time drug enforcement investigators, not part-time attention. Records and patterns which must be dealt with and reviewed daily require a familiarization standard which can only be achieved through specialization. Agencies refusing to accept the responsibility of dedicating full-time attention to the problem will fail to respond to the demands of the 1990s and will continue to reflect police organizational inefficiency. Agencies which have full-time drug enforcement assignments and offices have the basics from which to choose the principles from this map which will work best for their agency. Agencies generalizing their investigative work will simply have to tighten their belts and extend their specialization concepts.

The proper staffing of drug enforcement offices has always been a controversial topic within police circles. Administrators justifiably fear the affects of the work eroding some officers' integrity. A bigger fear has to do with assigning ill-equipped policemen to these functions to start with. Informal research into this issue has shown that the vast majority of drug enforcement officers who were adversely affected by the work, or who fell victim to corrupt influences, were officers who had propensities to digress from standard ethical requirements anyway, or who were emotionally deficient in dealing with the frustrations encountered in an assignment where progress is so rarely observable. In short, the assignment is simply not for everyone, and the most suitably equipped officers must be selected. Some agencies rotate officers in these assignments. That process sometimes works well; but, overall, the policy is self-defeating when the person assigned is properly equipped to perform the task and has the desire to continue in the assignment. Familiarity with patterns and suspects along with experience makes a drug enforcement detective valuable. Rotating detectives just to make sure they are not exposed **too much** to this type of work merely creates another poor management practice, causing low enthusiasm for the assignment in many police agencies. If rotation is necessary in a police agency because of past problems, then the practice may be justifiable in order to reinstate the proper tone. Otherwise, a procedure for closely monitoring warning signs that an investigator is affected by the assignment is sufficient.

Managers must be concerned with equipping the investigator with the proper training for drug investigation. The work calls for more than standard **detective training,** and more knowledge is required on areas such as handling informants and search-and-seizure issues. On-the-job training is often the only type of training afforded many small to mid-sized police department drug investigators. While OJT is a valued teacher, nothing replaces the benefits of formal instruction in the latest techniques. Without formal training, investigators are reduced to utilizing practices and procedures which may be outdated.

Principle Number 3: Asset Forfeitures. Paying for this drug enforcement strategy presents a major obstacle to small and mid-sized police agencies. For the next several years, federal funding should be available to practically every law enforcement agency in the country, producing at least a 50-50 match in funds. Planners need to accept the fact that, eventually, funding will be reduced and ultimately exhausted from the federal level. But this fact of budgeting should not influence long-term planning. Using federal funds effectively while they are available is the primary issue. When used effectively and in conjunction with an aggressive asset forfeiture program using laws designed to introduce court-ordered asset forfeiture back into the drug enforcement efforts, a perpetually budgeted drug strategy will be in place. This type of budgetary planning will underwrite a strategy long after the life of federal funding, and may further increase the likelihood of a long-term commitment from administrators and external politicians who are ultimately faced with stretching funds to budget even the most modest of strategies.

Each state has its own asset forfeiture laws, but another viable avenue is also open through which to initiate this principle. In 1984, federal legislation was enacted which authorized the U.S. Justice Department to share assets seized and awarded by the court with state and local law enforcement agencies which participated in the investigations and arrests. The U.S. Attorney General's Office predicted that $30 million in forfeiture awards would be shared with state and local police in 1988 alone. In 1987, the U.S. Justice Department approved payment of $24.4 million to state and local police agencies under this sharing policy. Federal task forces, comprised of state and local agencies, had seized cash and property valued at $495 million and had been awarded forfeitures from federal courts totaling $141 million in 1986.

Complaints accompany the program. Many police agencies argue that the process takes too long. In some cases, the wait for an award has taken months and even as long as two years, but planners should not allow these types of unavoidable and often bureaucratic delays to prevent them from initiating their programs.

Lexington, Kentucky's, police department is considered a mid-sized agency. The organization serves a population of around 250,000. There are 12 detectives who make up a four-agency task force assigned to the department's drug enforcement office. Over a recent 15-month period, that office was involved with the DEA in more than 50 cases which have netted seizures valued at over a half million dollars, all of which fall under the asset forfeiture sharing program. The office is in line to receive $300,000 of those seizures, in addition to what the office seized and has been awarded through state courts. As their strategy continues, additional asset forfeitures are being made which will be awarded down the road. In essence, this department's drug enforcement strategy is going to be funded for the next several years based on awarded asset forfeitures alone. As the awards are made, necessary equipment, vehicles, buy money, and operational expenses are budgeted. Eventually, the agency may even use awarded funds to offset the costs of additional personnel and, of course, to lessen the burden of the local government on overtime costs, always high in drug enforcement work.

Many planners may feel that a few hundred thousand dollars will not cure the ills or address the depth of the problems associated with drug availability in their areas. Perhaps not, but the funds, if used wisely, will provide seed money upon which to base a strategy which will increase the capabilities of an agency to underwrite an expanded strategy that will realistically address the depth of the problems. Properly budgeted awards can be the basis of matching funds for existing federal grants. The increasing evidence linking drugs to Part One crime rates opens new avenues and should provide new incentive for police managers to initiate aggressive asset forfeiture programs. Awarded funds are generally earmarked for drug enforcement efforts. However, if managers document their information to justifiably reflect, for example, that drug availability has directly influenced the homicide rate in their area, then some of these funds may be used to train homicide detectives or pay for overtime used by homicide detectives when investigating drug-related murders. Other areas in which awarded funds may be dedicated for a department-wide strategy and benefit are limited only by the lack of foresight by the police manager in the 1990s.

Ironically, drug enforcement has been the one area in which police

administrators have always voiced complaints and concerns about the
lack of funding. Those who continue to voice this concern are not
exploring or aggressively pursuing these types of perpetually funded
program concepts.

Principle Number 4: Reporting—Community and Officers. In order to
efficiently gauge drug availability and the community's desire to support strenuous drug enforcement efforts, a meaningful reporting system
must be established. The reporting system must not only be capable of
returning viable statistics on the types of complaints made, investigated,
and cleared, but also of categorizing those complaints in areas of drug
types, locations, suspect information, vehicles, and whether or not the
report was generated from the drug enforcement detectives, uniform
patrol, or the public. Close examination of the results of a reporting
system can reveal to police managers the most predominant drugs available in their areas, geographics concerning the offenses, and invaluable
suspect identification information.

Drug enforcement work is no different than other investigative processes
when it comes to informational resources. A strategy must address measures to assure reporting by the agency's uniformed officers and provide
a location where the general public may report information openly or
anonymously. The strategy must also include a procedure through which
uniformed officers are kept informed on the status of the information
reported. Interdepartmental surveys have revealed that most uniformed
officers possess plentiful information about suspected drug offenders
and their habits, but the information is rarely passed on or documented
for reference or cross indexing. The reason was found to be that officers
most frequently felt that their information did not receive attention.
They developed an attitude that reporting the information was not
worthwhile. The attitude is no different than the general public's attitude when information is reported but no results observed. To offset this
real or perceived problem, managers should require drug enforcement
investigators to respond to reporting officers within a fixed period of
time concerning the progress made on the information originally reported.
Even if the information submitted was only filed for reference, the
reporting officer should be informed and provided with justification for
filing the information. Fundamentally a good management, this response
reaps its own rewards. A brief memorandum suffices, and it increases the
probability that the officer will continue to report information observed
or learned.

Encouraging informational reporting from the public is not as difficult as it may appear. Police departments have used hot line concepts and even reward systems to encourage reporting. The programs work, but these special programs may be unnecessary as drugs continue to be in the forefront of issues and concerns of communities. An agency with a formal drug enforcement office will receive an abundance of reports from the general public in the form of telephone calls and letters. Planners must first evaluate the volume received through this informal approach before introducing new programs to increase the flow of necessary information into the enforcement office. Studies across the country have shown that fewer citizens seek rewards of any kind for reporting drug information as compared to those reporting offenses or suspect identities on Part One crimes. Planners may need only establish a reporting telephone number or numbers within their agency to accept and coordinate the calls concerning drug offenses. A reporting center must be identified to the public as part of the overall strategy. (Principle Number 9 will facilitate and expose the reporting center's purpose and access.)

Principle Number 5: Inclusion of Uniformed Officers in the Strategy. The era of centralizing the responsibility for enforcing drug laws has passed. Although specialized drug enforcement offices are a requisite for a successful strategy, an emphasis must be placed on decentralization and a more widespread involvement of department personnel in the primary enforcement assignment: uniform patrol. Uniformed officers must be incorporated into the strategy to provide an agency with the necessary strength to actually impact and deter drug availability. The uniformed patrol force has always been and will continue to be the most heavily staffed function in any police organization. It is plainly good management to utilize their presence to further enhance drug enforcement, but not take away from their other responsibilities and priorities.

The uniformed officer on patrol assignment comes into contact with and observes more activity in one tour of duty than most investigators do during an entire week. Their involvement in any agency-wide strategy is vital for this very reason. Planners must also realize that these are the officers who will eventually progress to be assigned to full-time drug enforcement offices, fulfilling a need for sorely needed experienced personnel to move into this expanding area. Officers with some experience, background, and involvement in drug enforcement work will certainly prove to be the most suitable candidates for full-time assignments in investigative offices, so the inclusion of uniform personnel in this area will pay future dividends to managers who must staff future drug enforcement offices.

The most modern patrol drug enforcement program is still in an infant stage. Courts are pondering cases, and indicators suggest that the courts will strengthen the capabilities of law enforcement to utilize the program widely known as selective drug patrol or criminal patrol drug enforcement. The concept has grown out of the widely used profiling techniques first developed by the Drug Enforcement Administration and U.S. Customs in the early 1970s. Profiling suspected drug offenders in airports slowly became another of law enforcement's informal sciences. The probabilities surrounding a person's actions, dress, mannerisms, and even their belongings during certain times and locations in an airport, provide drug agents with reasonable cause to believe a person may be a drug courier. The courts have never concluded that this informal profiling provides immediate probable cause for arrest, but the totality of the circumstances in each individual incident underscored the accuracy of informal profiling, and soon courts were affirming cases which were initially based upon profiling measures. Southern states were the first areas in the country to realize the benefits of patrol officers, primarily on interstate highways, using an adoptive informal profiling concept. State police in Florida, Georgia, and Louisiana (as well as other states through which north/south interstate systems run) developed their own profiling system based upon the frequency of similarities between the types of cars and descriptions of persons most often arrested on the interstates with quantities of drugs. From these informal findings, patterns began to emerge. It was soon realized that certain vehicles with certain state licenses were frequently found to be involved in drug transportation. Certain races, sexes, and ages of occupants in those vehicles further widened the possibilities. Times of the day, driving practices, and reactions of drivers upon seeing a marked police vehicle all became part of the informal profiling. The 1968 landmark Supreme Court case of Terry v. Ohio was the basis for the entire development of criminal patrol drug enforcement programs, and the courts continue to expand their recognition of the investigative stop as an intermediate response available to police engaged in investigating possible criminal activity when probable cause to arrest is absent. The simple difference between the elements of the Terry v. Ohio case and criminal patrol drug enforcement cases is that the cases today primarily take place on the streets and highways, which are the problems of the 1980s and 1990s, not the sidewalks and alleys where the problems existed in the 1970s.

Interdiction success from these early efforts led to the development of formal programs which expanded the techniques and profiling signals which are now being used in many areas across the country. The Institute of Police Technology and Management (IPTM) at the University of North Florida, Jacksonville, has developed a formal training course on criminal patrol drug enforcement. A recognized leader in police training, IPTM consolidates the courses to enable municipal, county, and state police agencies to combat the increasing transit of drugs through practical involvement and learning methods based on not only profiling, but the support subjects necessary for officers to fully utilize this new concept in their own jurisdictions. The overall concept and strategy trains uniformed officers in detection and apprehension of drug users and couriers, drug identification and investigation, vehicle search and seizure procedures, and preparation of testimony and evidence for court prosecution. The training emphasizes the use of interview techniques, and drug identification and recognition. Agencies which have exposed their uniformed officers to this formal training have increased their department's overall organization resources and are finding that their agencies are beginning to further disrupt drug availability.

An overall study of the effectiveness of this concept has not been compiled for the country, but the statistics from agencies practicing this advanced technique speak for themselves. In Louisiana, for example, a 12-month concentrated program by the state police resulted in over $1.5 million of currency seized, over $7.6 million in street valued drugs, 1,489 total apprehensions for various offenses in addition to drug arrests, and close to 5,000 field inquiries based upon stops. A total of 18 state police officers were involved in this project during the period. Police planners should be able to take this information and place it into perspective for their own jurisdictions and see the benefits of moving their agency in the direction by bottling up the avenues through which a majority of the illicit drugs in this country are transported.

Principle Number 6: Drug Detection Animals. Specialized investigators concentrate on long-term, quick response enforcement measures in this strategy plan. The use of patrol officers widens the emphasis and certainly broadens the deterrent elements necessary to decrease the availability of drugs. In order to extend the deterrent element into areas that are rarely efficiently addressed by long- or short-term investigation,

planners need to expand their strategy into the areas of drug importa-
tion and transportation. Even novice drug enforcement specialists recognize that drugs are imported and moved through a limited number of
conveyances, aircraft, motor vehicles, and boats. Disruption of those
distribution capabilities, the theory goes, will reduce drug availability.
But, as in most areas of endeavor, rarely do tough problems have simple
solutions. Although curbing the drug trade by cutting transportation
routes appears practical, 20 years of full-time drug enforcement efforts
have failed to significantly disrupt the staggering influx. Despite holes
in the theory, planners can readily identify and plug problem areas
through the use of drug detection animals. Expensive as they may be,
drug detection animals pay for themselves very quickly when used in a
systematic manner within an overall strategy. These highly trained animals cannot be effectively replaced with any other method under existing
laws and practices. A dog, for instance, provides an excellent proactive
program capability within the strategy to target overnight express services,
airline freight shipments, parcel services, and the heavily used delivery
services of the United States Post Office. A dog program also lends itself
to enhancing the effectiveness of search warrant executions as well as
giving patrol officers another resource through which to develop probable cause on any traffic stop or field inquiry made under a criminal
patrol drug enforcement program.

"Drug dog" programs must be systematically orchestrated to fit into
the strategy most effective for the agency. Many agencies have drug
detection animals, but few mandate a program which requires the animals to be used daily in planned programs designed to create the tone of
deterrence. Utilizing a dog only for call-out purposes diminishes the
effect of the principle and fails to make the most out of a precious piece
of equipment. A program designed to routinely, but in a nonpredictable
pattern, use the dog for walk-throughs of detention facilities, inspections
of overnight delivery services, and freight shipments at rental car
businesses ultimately will develop into a deterrent element as word
spreads of the predictable success. Coordinating programs which allow
walk-throughs in schools, some university areas, bus freight deliveries,
and perhaps even work places (upon the invitation of the management)
will soon highlight the serious deterrent impact this aggressive concept
can deliver. The animal cannot do the job unless the police planner
creates a program to its fullest capabilities. Successes from drug animal
detection programs receive quick support from communities which want

to see their police departments do more to thwart the availability of drugs in neglected areas.

Principle Number 7: Clear Responsibilities for the Drug Enforcement Officer. Traditionally, those agencies which have the luxury of staffing a full-time drug enforcement office have found that the office is made accountable for other crimes which police managers have often felt were directly linked to drug offenses. Many departments merge offices which investigate vice, alcohol beverage control, and organized crime into their drug enforcement function. While this may occasionally work effectively, many agencies want to bundle drug enforcement efforts with clumps of the other crimes which may or may not be linked with drug crimes. Caution should be exercised by police planners in the 1990s not to allow drug enforcement efforts to be overwhelmed or take a back seat to these associated crimes. Drug enforcement strategies require a concise and clear direction if they are to have an effective impact. The duties of the drug enforcement investigator should not be merged with the duties directly associated with that of a vice investigator. When and if vice crimes and drug crimes are both identified within an investigation, managers should view the occasion no differently than, for instance, a case of a homicide detective who encounters a burglary offense during the course of a death investigation. If the burglary circumstances are clearly a part of the homicide case, the homicide detective would normally proceed in handling both. Should the detective find that the burglary is unrelated, then it should be handled by a burglary detective, separate from the death investigation. Agencies which are limited in staffing their investigative branch will encounter problems on this principle; but, as stated, [to be a productive component of the agency], drug enforcement work must receive full-time attention. A written standard operating procedure designed to address the work of drug enforcement investigators will assist planners in developing the proper direction for their strategies.

Principle Number 8: Federal Funding. Drug enforcement funding from the Federal government will be available to all state and local police agencies in the closing years of the 1980s and for the first few years of the 1990s. While funds may be less for some jurisdictions, there still will be federal monies available to assist even the most modest strategy plan. Police organizations that fail to capitalize on the availability of grants will falter in their drug enforcement mission. Some police agencies never apply for grants in any area, often citing past frustrations stemming from inability to appropriate money to use as matching funds. In-kind grants are available through which the existing salaries or equipment to be used can be substituted for cash matches. The U.S. Justice Department also awards discretionary grants which require no matching funds. These types of grants are usually limited to a set amount and are based on program need, so practically all police agencies, regardless of size, are considered. Police agencies which are expecting asset forfeiture awards from previous cases, but have yet to receive the cash to use as a match, may also in some circumstances use this anticipated award in the place of cash-on-hand for a match.

Funding drug enforcement strategies will require managers who are responsible for the function to become fiscal officers in addition to their other duties. Administrators and managers planning for future strategies most recognize the need for a fiscal plan through which asset forfeiture accounts can be managed. Managers must become thoroughly familiar with grant availability, grant writing, and grant administration if an agency is going to take advantage of the seed monies which will initially become the foundation for drug enforcement in the 1990s.

Principle Number 9: Visability and Coordination with the Media. The most effective, productive, efficient, and workable drug enforcement strategy implemented will not work at all if police managers fail to include a method of assuring that the achievements of the strategy are made known to the community. The lack of this final principle results in the immediate loss of all deterrent values and the inconsistent support of the public in future drug enforcement actions. Planners must publicize their agency's achievements in accordance with their overall strategy plan.

Premature publicity surrounding a criminal patrol drug enforcement program may produce problems similar to the premature announcement that a drug dog is going to walk through a detention facility every Monday at 9 a.m. Common sense in applying this principle will not only maintain a higher level of public confidence, but will also set the tone for more cooperative reporting of drug offenses by the public, thus increasing the effectiveness of Principle Number 4. Media coverage of drug issues will not have to be encouraged by police planners for the next several years. Planners should take advantage of this interest by the media and coordinate a purposeful program which keeps the public informed of not only the achievements but also the real levels of the problems and what needs to be done to address those problems in the future.

Element B: The Drug Education and Awareness Strategy

Past Strategy Concept and Their Failures. In the early and mid-1970s, many law enforcement planners recognized that enforcement of drug laws by itself would never curb drug availability and use. Curtailing the supply through interdiction alone was a noble approach and, unfortunately, a more ambitious undertaking than a police service could handle. Those responsible on the front line for drug enforcement programs encouraged the adoption and expansion of drug education and awareness programs for their communities. Most programs were disjointed and primarily presented through public and community relations personnel who were more adept at presentations about traditional police topics like driver safety, prevention of sex crimes, and shoplifting. Hand-out materials were usually pamphlets left over from the late sixties, or poorly edited, reprinted versions of the same type of information about drugs that had been used in preceding years in the nation's half-hearted attempt to inform the public about the **dangers of drug abuse.** Practically every piece of printed material and a majority of the films used in drug education programs at the time were predicated upon one instructional concept: the scare tactic. While this tactic may have proven somewhat effective in the more innocent decades of the fifties and early sixties, the same messages conveyed in the 1970s lacked credibility to the two target groups: young adults and preteens. Police speakers found their presentations scoffed at by youngsters who were immediately able to see that the message simply boiled down to **don't use drugs, because they'll kill you.** This singular message was hardly applicable to prevalent attitudes and to the street and cultural scenes of the 1970s. Obviously, people were dying from drugs, but most of rural and small-town America, a significant purchasing agent for drugs, was not witnessing or associating all drugs with death. Urban audiences may have seen death result from drug abuse, but marijuana and other "social drugs" were more acceptable and, in some major cities, as deeply embedded sociologically as alcohol consumption. The wave of radicalism associated with the late 1960s still permeated the main user groups of the 1970s; drugs continued to be associated with **causes** such as antiwar sentiments and disgust with political systems, all underlined by what some social scientists still see as the primary proponent of drug use at the time: music.

Regardless of the reasons behind the continued ignoring of the messages being delivered by police and other groups who attempted to educate the public about the dangers of drug abuse, early drug education efforts were a grand effort but a miserable failure. Drug availability was rampant. There are two reasons for the continued escalation: ineffective interdiction strategies, and the inability of drug education messages to reduce the acceptability of drug usage. The second reason directly influenced the demand for drugs. As the demand grew, interdiction strategies faltered and fell further behind.

As the 1970s came to a clash, another generation of potential drug users was emerging. Most law enforcement groups accepted the failures of the past programs, and scare tactics were abandoned to be the main theme of the organized programs. New information, new materials, new films, and a more conservative national tone was influencing the way most people viewed drugs and their abuse. Law enforcement officials who had struggled with enforcement and education programs understood the necessity of formulating a long-range educational program which would divert the social acceptability of drugs and move away from the attempts to find and introduce a quick fix to the problem. A new era in drug education philosophy was emminent, and a more workable alternative was developed. But the new approach would face detractors because the philosophy was a long-term approach, and there would be no immediate results.

Project DARE. The development of this new educational approach was based on the findings that drug education needed to be more than mere admonishments. Youngsters, in particular, had to learn how to avoid and resist peer pressures. Officials also had to accept the fact that at least two generations had been lost to drug abuse and, possibly, a third would be damaged. The new philosophy targets the age groups made up of the future. Focusing on children 7 to 14 appears to be the most effective route, but refining the age groups even lower may prove to have more of an impact 10 and 15 years down the road. The National Institute on Drug Abuse figures that 72 percent of the nation's estimated 45.3 million elementary and secondary school students are offered some form of drug education, but often that education only amounts to a paragraph in a health textbook.[18] This approach is inefficient. In order to effectively impact a group, programs must be continuous, not a guest speaker approach or a one-week **drug awareness** proclamation program designed to give brief attention to the issues and topic. A program has to go beyond drugs and teach children about self-esteem and how to deal with the tensions and strains associated with peer pressure without turning to drugs.[19] Alternatives to drug use and misuse, safety, positive and negative consequences, and taking a stand must all be included in a curriculum organized within the nation's school system where peer pressure is most dominant. And it must start in the lower grades, even kindergarten. Children under the age of 10 or 12 are the one group in which nonuse of drugs, alcohol, and tobacco is the norm.[20] This is where true drug education must start, and it has started, first in California by the Los Angeles Police Department. The LAPD introduced the comprehensive DARE (Drug Abuse Resistance Education) program through that city's school system in 1983, arousing high hopes for the most influential drug education program ever conceived in the United States. Since 1983, the LAPD has expanded the program into 55 elementary schools. Project DARE is the best education strategy for the 1990s. Combined with meaningful and practical enforcement strategy principles as set forth in Element A, police organizations may reach the ultimate goal of reducing drug availability through sound enforcement measures supported by diminishing demand.

The primary objection to the use of this type of long-range strategy originates from those who want action now. It is popularly forecasted that police administrators in the 1990s will begin to see the expected results of the overall enforcement-education strategy. Those administrators are the planners and managers who are now in positions to develop these efforts.

Since 1983, over 60 school districts in the United States have adopted the DARE program. Under the DARE concept, police officers use 17 different lessons during a semester to teach the foundations upon which DARE lessons are based. Actually, DARE lessons have little to do with drugs as an individual topic. The lessons focus on self-esteem, the tensions of growing up in a peer pressure setting, and other vital decision-making processes, all illustrated through role playing to point out the underlying ability of each child to resist drugs. The project emphasizes the value of taking a stand and eventually culminates in a reverse peer pressure situation, making it more popular not to abuse drugs than to abuse them. Uniquely, this project involves police officers, in uniform, actually being absorbed into the certified teaching curriculum of a school system. These officers are exposed to DARE training programs which certify their instructional abilities to teach these lessons.

The Necessary Commitment. Communities which have adopted the DARE projects are giving rave reviews to the new attitudes of their children, not only toward drugs but to the extension of mature reasoning in dealing with other pressures of adolescence. It is usually the police agency involved in the actual instruction that receives the most praise. Obviously, commitment must be made on the part of police agencies to this long-term education program, a commitment in training, manpower, and the ideals of the project. The program is one that must be exposed to as many students in the age brackets established as long as possible. A two- or three-year commitment will not work. Planners must understand and realize that an entire generation could create the demand for drugs in the future. The more members of that generation who are exposed to the types of lessons afforded in the DARE project, the less the demand will increase during the generation's peak user period.

Evaluations of this program are ongoing across the country. Most are set up on five-year periods. That control time should be enough to accurately forecast the effectiveness of the concept. Authorities, parents, and educators who have been involved and exposed to the program contend that the effectiveness will be overwhelming. Widespread DARE programs, along with the other inevitable influences of sociological change over the next several years, could lead to a lessening in the demand from this generation. In order to reap the benefits of this program in the 1990s in any community, large or small, planners must start now to incorporate the project into their drug strategies and to obtain the commitment necessary for the project to work.

Planners may find that speaking directly to officers who teach and to managers directly involved in existing DARE programs may be a beneficial avenue for research into developing a DARE project. Ideas for grant funding and organizational placement and allotment of manpower are best obtained from direct sources. The LAPD has the most experience and is the largest agency using the DARE concepts. The Lexington, Kentucky, Division of Police has the most progressive evaluation process being undertaken of the DARE program. Research into both departments' program design, funding, training, and evaluations of their projects would be worthwhile.

VICTIMS IN THE CRIMINAL JUSTICE SYSTEM

The 1980s will be the decade accredited for most advancing the awareness of police agencies to the key role played by crime victims and the necessity of doing more for the victim through the criminal justice system. Research shows that the crime victim is most important in helping police identify and apprehend offenders. Crime victims are finally being seen as main players; not only in the efforts to apprehend offenders, but in consistent and vigorous prosecution as well. New studies have helped reshape police thinking in this area, and police agencies are seeing another role emerging from these new considerations—the role of police response to victims through the development of programs which assure that the trauma of being a victim is addressed properly through referral to social services and, in some cases, direct financial compensation.

The Necessity of a More Focused Attention

National attention has been focused on crime victims since the early 1980s. A National Crime Victims Week has been proclaimed by the President annually since 1982; and the 1982 Omnibus Victim and Witness Protection Act, along with the 1984 Comprehensive Crime Control Act and the Victims of Crime Act, establishes the tone for a new attitude. Federal legislation introduced the use of victim impact statements at sentencing in federal courts. It gave federal judges the authority to order restitution from offenders to victims, and outlined additional measures to assure greater protection of crime victims and witnesses from intimidation by an offender or by friends of an offender. Federal funds appropriated under the 1984 act are used to compensate crime victims for expenses which came about because they were victimized by a criminal. Since 1984, more than 36 states have enacted legislation which further protects crime victims and, in some cases, provides financial compensation for expenses such as medical bills.

Many prosecution offices across the country have adopted special programs to coordinate victims' assistance benefits and referrals. The efforts arose from findings that most crime victims did not realize that such benefits were available to them. Prosecutors' offices have, within the past few years, instituted measures which make involvement in trials and hearings more acceptable to victims and witnesses, and compensated them for time away from their jobs and loss of pay.

Laws Governing Victims' Rights

The enactment of the 1984 Victims of Crime Act (VOCA) heralded a new era for services to crime victims.[21] The act gave national attention to the National Organization for Victim Assistance (NOVA), a nationwide association of supporters and victims or family members of crime victims. NOVA sponsors national conferences to further public awareness of the crime victim's position, and the association was partially responsible for the initial funding of Federal monies dedicated to support the 1984 act. The act is a good example of making criminals pay for their crimes. Fines and forfeitures from earmarked cases are deposited into compensation programs and local victim assistance services. As of 1988, there is a $110 million ceiling on this particular fund. NOVA sponsors national conferences to further public awareness and support of the act and various programs. It is clear that VOCA and NOVA have advanced victim rights throughout the nation. VOCA grants stimulate state spending in various programs designed to assist crime victims and create proactive, new programs such as domestic violence units in many police agencies. The matching grant funds available resulted in over $250 million being expended through these state programs in over 38 states.

The Police Role

In addition to recognizing the need to enhance the VOCA concept, police planners should become familiar with the Federal funding available in this area to underwrite projects and programs which would further enhance the police mission of the 1990s. Planners should consider the value of using VOCA guidelines to finance enforcement directions in the areas of domestic violence and crimes against children offenses. The planner for the 1990s will realize that funds for these types of services and enforcement may be available from VOCA grants, possibly allowing a rededication of locally budgeted funds to other programs. Agencies failing to examine the true necessity of victim assistance type programs for their communities will be tragically remiss in the 1990s. As the nation moves toward more emphasis on victims' rights, police planners need to look ahead at areas of enforcement and services they may provide to their communities that will keep their agencies attuned to issues which most concern their citizens. The police agency that productively uses available federal funding now in this area will be more adept to the victim rights issues in the latter part of the 1990s. As the issue grows, the ways in which these programs will assist police in all areas of enforcement will improve.

Planners should consider the value of being involved in victim assistance program development. A coordinator may work best from the agency's community service office or perhaps their criminal investigation office in conjunction with a local prosecutor's office.

HOSTAGE NEGOTIATIONS AND TACTICAL INCIDENT MANAGEMENT

The rash of skyjackings in the United States in the late 1960s paved the way for the tactic to be recognized as a means to sensationalize political positions, bargain for media exposure, and demonstrate commitment to certain factionalized views. Hostage-taking during this period frequently took the form of political kidnappings which further exposed the tactic as an effective terrorist tool. The 1970s saw a different tactic rise in the United States. The political activist no longer held a monopoly on hostage-taking. The larger cities in the country were first to experience the change. Criminals barricaded themselves in houses, apartments, or businesses where they had committed or were committing crimes and were suddenly caught in the act. Emotionally disturbed people frequently attracted attention and vented their frustrations by barricading themselves or holding family members or others hostage. As with any new problem experienced by the police, departments fell back on known frames of reference to handle these situations, soon giving birth to Special Weapons and Tactics (SWAT) teams. These teams were comprised of officers employing massive firepower and commonly used strict military tactics, but it was soon realized that SWAT teams often worsened the situation. Potential suicides, for instance, frequently explode with not only the death of the potential suicide victim, but with unnecessary gunfire being exchanged. Public criticism and civil suits dampened law enforcement's enthusiasm to continue to deal with these incidents through the measures employed by SWAT teams.

The Evolution of the Need

The New York Police Department experimented with new techniques in handling these situations in the early 1970s. The department's program led to successful negotiations with potential suicide victims, criminals, political activists, and the emotionally disturbed. The term **hostage negotiation** was coined by the NYPD, and their techniques were instrumental in the emergence of procedures for police departments across America, including the FBI, in other parts of the world. The NYPD learned quickly that talk and a systematic way of gathering information about the person or group involved is the fundamental key to successful negotiations. This format and a no-nonsense, formal procedure outlining the use and deployment of tactical units or squads in conjunction to the negotiations increased the probability of success. As this program and as others across the country began to evolve, it was recognized early that police departments must train officers to immediately recognize and identify possible hostage or barricade situations and to exercise firearm discipline when confronting the situation. The first officers on the scene are likely to set the tone for the negotiations to follow. Violence at the initial phase could set a pro-violence atmosphere and unsuccessful negotiations. Backing off, guarding the perimeter of the incident area, and waiting for the negotiators more often proves to calm the offender and establish a smoother path to a dialogue with the offender or suspect.

As experience in this relatively new area of law enforcement response grew, critiques and analyses of each incident pinpointed problems, developed new approaches, and created comparative criteria for future use. The roles of the first officer and the uniform patrol supervisor at the scene, deployment of additional personnel, handling the media, and the type of equipment necessary to have on hand (ranging from communications equipment to chemical agents and food), all began to surface in operating guide books. The experiences also provided information for planners on the necessity of a selection criteria for negotiators and for officers assigned to the tactical unit. Training was seen as a key requirement and, depending on the size of the department, units and offices were established through which to manage negotiation and tactical teams.

Consideration of Forecasts and Predictions

Since the 1970s, tactical incidents no longer are exclusively found in the larger urban areas. Even the smallest communities experience hostage, suicide, and barricade incidents. As the police service moves into the 1990s, managers in large, mid-sized, and smaller departments must plan on this topic. The Delphi Study forecasts a rise in terrorism incidents in the country by the year 1995 and discusses probable civil unrest by the end of that decade. Those doubting the forecasts may want to examine another avenue in consideration in their planning. Cut in half these two predictions. Believe that the predictions will take place, but in only half of the severity level forecasted. Now, planners should ask themselves if their agency is prepared to handle an incident even at half the level of the predictions. Those planners doubting their agency's ability to han dle the types of problems forecasted need to get busy on this topic. Planners should also understand that while no one predicts terrorist activities to immediately take place in small rural areas, hostage situations may still arise. Planners should also consider that when skyjacking and political kidnapping first started being reported and witnessed in the 1960s, few people predicted that the actions would give rise to the other types of incidents that the police have handled in the last two decades. Planners should take into account the probability of carry-over or copy-cat incidents.

Rethinking the Concept

Many state police agencies have negotiation and tactical teams which are used in rural settings where police agencies are small and cannot afford the luxury of their own teams. Mobilization and the time it takes to respond is a key concern planners should consider if they are going to continue using this approach in the 1990s. Large or mid-sized departments may find that the use of teams may require a different organizational method in the 1990s. Many departments now use call-outs to form their teams. The team members may be assigned to various duties through a police agency; but when an incident takes place, they are mobilized into one team under a different command structure. Depending on geographics, the 1990s may call for a rethinking of this procedure.

Smaller agencies may find it more useful to plan and manage incidents through a mutual aid agreement with other police agencies in their immediate vicinity. This planning could be used by townships and smaller municipalities where a combination of aid could reduce mobilization time and even cut costs. Obviously, a formal, legally acceptable agreement would be required between the various agencies participating. The agreement could be extended beyond tactical incidents and address natural disasters or other cases of local peril which may be considered a **state of emergency.** Command, training, formal, and periodic mobilization exercises would be addressed in a formal agreement, as well as liability issues. As any planner knows, this approach has built-in bureaucratic obstacles, but it's not impossible; and, in order to explore the various avenues and adopt a program which is suitable for individual communities, planners must start now in order to be prepared for the 1990s.

Research by planners who are either developing a program or looking to strengthen their existing program is necessary. There are numerous tactical incidents across the country each month. The accumulated experiences total a wealth of information upon which planners and managers can more effectively develop their own department's capabilities in dealing with these incidents.

Police service has always reflected the most entrenched American middle-class values and has, therefore, faced criticism and attack from those who represent other values.[22] There are few areas in law enforcement as open to scrutiny as the tactical incident. Proper tactical response is extremely complicated, and law enforcement cannot chance being perceived by their communities as brutal, vicious, or disorganized. The impact of an improperly handled situation can be so overwhelming that the after-incident publicity may be more devastating than the actual tactical deployment.

Many police agencies view their tactical and negotiation teams as a special function assigned to respond to special problems which uniformed officers on the beat are not trained to effectively handle. Although this one-dimensional view is accurate up to a point, planners and managers for the 1990s must see that the special response that has been developed and that will continue to be fine-tuned is actually a spark of insurrection of police attitudes. Values of the police service are changing, and these concepts of genuine concern exemplified through the efforts and evolution of tactical incident management are carrying over into other areas of police service.[23]

SETTING A FUTURISTIC MANAGEMENT TONE
FOR THE 1990S

No simple formulae exist for planners to use when addressing the need to revolutionize police management thinking in the 1990s. Instituting measures which may result in a change of management philosophy may be the only course available in the last decade of this century. External factors will cause some management philosophy changes, but internally planners will be capable of at least identifying the psychological mines that will be encountered, as well as the psychological blocks to innovation and creativity within the police organization. Once identified, planners must devise ways to train up-and-coming managers to avoid these pitfalls and to constantly be on the alert for other mines and blockages of the development of futuristic management concepts.

Psychological Blocks

Authorities have long since determined that there are certain psychological blocks that hinder people from developing creative and innovative ideas. The following four blocks must be removed within police management:

1. STATUS ENDANGERMENT: Whenever someone comes up with a new idea, that person endangers his or her present status. Doing things that have not been done before will brand a person as not being satisfied with the status quo, and the reaction of fellow officers could stifle their desire to be creative in certain organizational settings.

2. THE NEED FOR PERSISTENCE: Most innovators fail repeatedly before success is ultimately achieved. An organization which fails to remove or at least lessen the impacts of STATUS ENDANGERMENT as a result of failure will immediately falter because officers won't take chances.

3. THE NEED FOR TIME: Every manager working in every field is under the pressure of time. Managers sometimes cannot wait for creativity and innovation, and must go on with what they have at the time. In police service, change as a result of creativity and innovation often comes at a slow pace. The pitfall here is that managers who are forced to move on with what they have may get

into that habit, again stifling creativity and innovation because it will appear that nothing suggested is ever put into effect.

4. THE NEED FOR NEW FRAMES OF REFERENCE: To innovate or create something new requires that managers put away old ways of looking at problems, situations, or ideas, because previous frames of reference block people from seeing something new.[24]

Top Executive Performance

William H. Cohen and Nurit Cohen presented these four blocks in their 1984 book, **Top Executive Performance.** They dedicate an entire chapter on ways managers can overcome these blocks in order to advance their organizations... the principles apply to any organization. Other principles are offered by the Cohens in methods managers can use to start seeing old problems in new ways. These principles are a treasure chest of information for police planners, and again underscore the need for police managers to look beyond traditional police texts for solutions to police management problems.

Blending Modern Management Science with Police Management

One of the most powerful lessons to be learned is that no matter how well equipped an organization may be, the final result will be closely tied to the skill and thoroughness of planning that went before.[25] The 1990s will be time for training managers and leaders for the next century, and there will undoubtedly be an array of processes touted by various training institutes to provide law enforcement with formal classroom training for this purpose. Cracks in the officer development system will still exist over the next decade, even if training and formal instruction begin to fit the bill. But some measures can be incorporated now by planners in anticipation of the leadership development which will be required. Planners are expected to separate the long-held contention that police management is different than the management of other types of organizations. The fundamentals are the same; only the product is vastly different. As a more enlightened police administration and management corp emerges during the next decade, a shift toward a more compatible management style will take place, a style similar to those in most major industries and some public organizations. Advancements and changes will, of course, take place, and continuing adjustments in management style will probably surface before the end of the next decade in these other organizations. Sticking with old police management methods, law enforcement schools may retard advancements, but most are expected to broaden their instructional views and present more harmonious teachings based on modern management sciences. To cement some of the cracks which will still exist, planners can look toward private institutes for management lessons which offer supervision, management, and leadership seminars as a form of special tutoring and exposure of their personnel to the current management science practices of other organizations. There are costs associated with using these seminars, which last from eight hours to a week, but costs may generally be offset by sending more than one person at a time or a group of newly promoted officers. The innovative approach of sending patrol officers who aspire to supervisory levels enhances later assessment of testing processes. Most of these private institutes will design special programs on specific topics for specific organizations, an invaluable tool to police service in that professionals can address problem-oriented management conflicts which specifically haunt law enforcement agencies while infusing a strong dose of modern management practices.

The smaller law enforcement agency may face funding problems which prohibit the use of private management institutions. If police egos and certain types of rivalries can be put aside, a smaller agency may find that by inviting a larger agency to create and conduct a supervision or management course, they could acquire some knowledge which may advance their agency without costing their governing body a cent. Intra-agency pride usually prevents this type of meaningful exchange between police departments through the country, but it is another angle that needs to be explored by the planner.

Police agencies have always bent over backwards to help other police agencies in practically every aspect of law enforcement except open-armed exchanges which can advance management practices. This concept is not restricted to the scenario of the small department asking the larger department for instruction. Any department should be able to ask another agency to present formal instruction on a variety of administrative, management, or supervision topics which have been found to work best without claims that one department's style is the **only solution** or is better than another. Planners should realize that exposure to new concepts and the way other people make things work is the real force behind change and learning at all levels. Consider the long-range benefits of one agency calling upon another to prepare a **sharing of information** on what works best when dealing with specific management problems. That type of noncompetition atmosphere between agencies could be extended to other areas of mutual concern resulting in the marketing of ideas, direction, and planning for the future in concert with long-range development of police service.

There are several associations on the state and national level for police administrators. A few exist for fraternal purposes only, but others do and have made strides in bringing together top police officials across the country on a variety of issues. Interdepartmental training appears to be a concept that will not be taken through association efforts soon; therefore, mid-level managers today may be in the best position to further explore the development of this type of imaginative approach of interlacing police organizations through formal or informal settings of instruction and seminars.

THE ORGANIZATIONAL AUTOPSY

As police service undergoes metamorphosis due to both external and internal elements, planners will be in a position to examine and learn from the mistakes of not only the distant past, but the more recent years. Planners should be able to perform an autopsy of sorts on their respective agency's practices, leadership problems or strengths, and other areas which can assist in the restructuring of law enforcement's **frame of reference.** Since law enforcement management has no overall governing code of ethics under which strict accountability is set for all police service, the initial incision for this autopsy must be in the region of the organization, the core of police service evolution and change: decision-making and leadership. Once examined, these areas may suggest that a standard be more narrowly defined. All police service planners should keep in mind society's acceptance of the certain principles which define true professionalism but are still absent for police service.

The following 12 areas are not presented for substitution of what may be needed in order to prepare an overall law enforcement code of ethics. The areas are emphasized so that planners may check their organization's decision-making processes and leadership ethics as they make that initial incision.

Fredrick Lewis Donaldson summarized what he called the seven deadly sins of modern society in the following terms:

- Policies without principles
- Wealth without work
- Pleasure without conscience
- Industry without morality
- Knowledge without character
- Science without humanity
- Worship without sacrifice

The concepts may provide some insight and an understanding of some of society's ethical problems today, but there is an obvious lack of specificity that planners need in order to directly relate ethical concepts to police service.

Leadership Ethics

James J. Cribbin compiled a more contemporary ledger of ethical standards in 1981 which is more suitable for police planners when considering the presence or absence of decision-making and leadership ethics in their agencies.

1. Do not perform an action unless you would be willing to have it become a law binding all mankind.
2. Never use another person as a mere means to your personal ends nor permit anyone to use you in this manner.
3. Before engaging in a given behavior, ask yourself, **Would I be willing to justify my action before an objective, competent board of inquiry?**
4. Would you perform the act if you were certain that it would be on the 6 o'clock news?
5. How would you judge the action that you propose to take if it were done by your worst enemy?
6. If you excuse yourself on the grounds that everybody's doing it, would you do it if no one else did?
7. How would you feel if, after you had performed the proposed act, you were forced to justify your motives and behaviors to your children?
8. Would you be content if your superiors and associates were to behave toward you as you propose to act toward someone else?
9. Since people learn what they live and little else, would you be

willing to have each of your subordinates act in the precise manner that you intend?

10. If you feel that the pressures are too great to resist, how would you judge the behavior of a person competing against you who used the same justification?
11. If you reason that the damage done someone else by your behavior is small, what would your judgments be if everyone in your organization behaved in a similar way?
12. If you were to make a habit of doing what you propose to do, what kind of person would you become?[26]

The questions reveal the no-nonsense standards which any organization could adopt in some fashion. It is a good place for police planners to start when giving thought to setting a futuristic management tone in their respective agencies.

Six Fatal Flaws of Police Management

In further review of law enforcement's traditional threads of deficiencies in this area, planners may recognize seven of the fatal errors which are consistently absent. Actually, some of these flaws are seen throughout other leadership and decision-making processes in private industry and business, but the difference is that other organizations have been actively making strides in reducing these types of flaws in their management systems.

Fatal Flaw Number 1: Failure to Maintain a Sense of the Outside World.[27] This flaw must be corrected before all others can be influenced or changed. Leaders with little or no sense of how the police service fits into the scheme of modern society are going to be lost in the next decade when community involvement, based upon contemporary issues influenced by outside spheres or other problems not immediately seen within the community, will be in the forefront serving as a catalyst for more changes in law enforcement. National events and even world events shape reactions from law enforcement and have an impact on future planning regardless of the size of the agency. A simple example can be seen through the effects of Supreme Court decisions. Each decision influences police work to a degree. The decisions made by the Court are a result of nine individual viewpoints which may be weighted by current political theories as well as the Constitution. Law enforcement officials can easily see the need in this setting to have a sense of the outside world, and to be familiar with how the outside world will influence their environment. There exist numerous other outside influences, and planners for the future will have to be alert on how issues or events may shape law enforcement in the future.

Having a sense of the outside world also translates into being more familiar with the elements in Fatal Flaw Number 6.

Fatal Flaw Number 2: Wanting to be Liked, Not Respected as a Leader.[28] As police leadership evolves during the next decade, this flaw may become less of a problem than it has been in the past. While it may be important for a police leader to be liked, it is not a requisite. However, being respected is mandatory. Once educated and open-minded police managers become the majority in law enforcement, this flaw will loosen its grip in the scheme of organizational frames of reference for the younger managers for the next era. Planners need to view this flaw very seriously, and closely examine ways in which it inhibits true progress in their organizations. Leaders who strive to be liked rather than respected make bad decisions on behalf of the organization. Discipline in their areas of responsibility will be conspicuously lax, and a **good old boy** syndrome will be readily identifiable among their subordinates. Tough decisions rarely are made by this type of leader. People in leadership positions who attempt to manage in spite of this flaw will be less suitably equipped to lead in the 1990s, and the continued practice of this flaw will retard progress and serve as an undesirable example for future leaders to observe.

Fatal Flaw Number 3: Failures Make Problems Line Up One-By-One.[29] Amateur leaders often try to take on all of the problems at the same time, rarely handling any effectively. In dealing with crises, police management often passes problems down the chain of command until a majority land on the lower echelon positions. Even if problems are not passed down in this manner, a lower echelon leader will have all the problems he can handle through the normal course of events, without additional burdens being funneled down the chain of command.

Prioritizing and lining up problems so that they can be addressed in an organized manner reduces the likelihood of successful and effective resolution. As planners can see, experience and training can be used to attack this freshman leader syndrome. Unless life threatening, there are few situations which cannot be lined up, identified properly, and addressed through the fundamental process of decision-making. Upper echelon leaders must exemplify this process in the 1990s in order for the lower echelon leaders to learn and profit from this method. By prioritizing and making problems line up, leaders usually find more time for input on decisions from the very people those decision will impact, thus forming the foundation of participatory management processes. Decisions made under this prioritization approach also lessen resistance to change.

Fatal Flaw Number 4: Failure to Develop Capabilities to Deal with People Problems Versus Technical Problems.[30] For long-term effectiveness, leaders must accomplish work by being sensitive to the needs of those who work for and with them. Short-term results flourish in the atmosphere of autocratic styles of management, but inevitably failure for the individual leader and organization follows. In spite of planners observing this practice in today's police service, it is doubtful that a leader can be found who doesn't claim that he is **people-oriented.** Most police leaders possess the fundamental technical knowledge which drives the organization; they know how their agency works, but fail to understand that it is the people who get the organization where it wants to go. If the people in the agency do not cooperate or don't understand where the agency wants to go, the agency stalls and goes nowhere. More emphasis must be placed on developing and maintaining a productive relationship between leaders and their subordinates at all levels, not just the top levels.

Fatal Flaw Number 5: Failure to Keep Abreast of Developments in the Criminal Justice Field.[31] This flaw is closely related to Fatal Flaw Number 1, but addresses internal factors more than external. There exist many criminal justice and law enforcement periodicals, newsletters, and video summary tapes which provide leaders with the latest strategies, statistical information, and developments in the field. Many address specifics and dedicate themselves to special areas of interest such as drug enforcement, traffic, computer technology, record-keeping, community service programs, and even management. Many have moved their focus from fraternalistic type publications which appeared in the late 1960s and early 1970s, and have become valuable resources from which leaders can learn what is going on in other departments across the country. An increase in reading material and references provides a more rounded view of law enforcement in the United States, but it has also forced planners to painfully recognize how far behind their organizations may be when compared to other police departments. Some agencies distribute required reading lists for their leaders and for officers in speciality assignments from these publications, exposing more managers and potential future leaders to the advances and emerging concepts being touted. Planners should again recognize that one of the requirements for being a successful leader is making time to sit, read, study, and learn more about the task . . . and the field.[32] The more exposure, the more ideas and fertilization of the growth process.

Fatal Flaw Number 6: Failing to Avoid the Search for an Easy Answer. Everyone searches for easy answers; but when managers are seduced by processes that are not focused on organizational problems, an unbalanced view of what can be accomplished with a single program or a new approach sometimes dominates better judgment.[33] Planners may be able to think back on programs which were oversold and the implementation proved disappointing. Once this happens, the organization is sometimes required to defend the program or approach due to its substantial investment of resources and perhaps money.

A dynamic reversal of progress arises from this flaw. The future-minded, educated, and motivated planner may become so enamored by new techniques and skills that they begin to look for situations in which to put their knowledge to use. Noel Tichy and Mary Ann Davanna examined this phenomena in their book, "The Transformational Leader." Their research revealed that this era's talented, up-and-coming leaders often stumble over their own knowledge as they rush through the rapid advancements of managerial skills touted by many private businesses and industries. The result is the **little boy with the hammer phenomenon:** If you give a little boy a hammer, he proceeds under the false assumption that everything broken can be fixed by hammering it.[34]

Tichy and Davanna state that when managers are exposed to the managerial grid, quality circles, zero-based budgeting, dimensions of excellence, or strategic planning portfolio analysis, the risk is that they will try to use their new knowledge to solve all organizational ills. Although police service has not yet been accused of being this advanced in management application processes, the parallel is obvious. As younger, more educated police managers evolve and rise through the organizational structure, the temptation to apply some new and innovative approaches will be overwhelming, particularly when those approaches have already been proven in the private sector. The dangers, however, are still there, and police managers in this situation may find that they have been seduced and their focus is not on the organizational problems at all.

Planners can avoid seduction and, at the same time, develop yet another requirement for management in their policy structuring. To prevent "hammering," the following guidelines need to be in place:

1. Have an agenda. Planners must have an organizational anchor of sorts, one that will keep their problems in focus.
2. The organization's tone should reflect the understanding that there are no easy answers. Band-Aid® solutions should not be used on bleeding problems.
3. Balance the views offered in seeking solutions. Oversell is usually required to make change in organizations which are not used to change, but planners should never over-advocate their proposed solutions without the necessary balances in place.[35]

POLITICS AND POLICE LEADERSHIP

Never a completely comfortable relationship, police and politicians often seem destined to remain at odds over a variety of issues on several levels of law enforcement. The problems were immediately recognizable as modern police organizations developed back at the turn of the century, but few police administrations in the country have been able to distance themselves from adverse political influence. It appears, however, that in the future, politics could serve as a tool for planners, especially police chiefs who subscribe to the forward-thinking concepts of community-oriented policing.

The Relationship

Studies in the late 1970s supplied bleak views of the qualifications of top police leadership across the country. One such study determined that only 10 percent of the police chiefs in the country at that time held a bachelor's degree. Ten years later, a follow-up study revealed that almost 50 percent of these officials who led police departments with 75 or more full-time employees still did not possess a baccalaureate degree. Comparing that to heads of other organizations, it was found that 81 percent of chief executives held at least a bachelor's degree in 1980, and 41 percent had earned a graduate level degree.[36] Figures may prove somewhat higher for law enforcement in the next decade, but the underlying reasons for poor political relationships may be found in these existing figures. As pointed out by Donald Whitham in his studies of police executives and reform measures in 1986, it is probable that political leaders prefer to appoint police executives with low qualifications, perhaps because these types of police administrators are believed to be easier to control and manipulate. Political appointments do give rise to the indebtedness factors that come with political favors. Obviously, the problem must be examined on the qualifications and procedure of selection processes used in various jurisdictions before an outright indictment of this method can be established. However, most planners probably know an organization which has been affected by this theory.

Political Responsibilities

Whitham's studies contend that police administrators have failed in realizing that their positions entail **political responsibilities** as well as administrative duties. This consideration may well prove to be the pivotal logic required for police executives in the 1990s in order to become more effective in dealing with the political influences that are sure to continue to impact law enforcement well into the next century. Police chiefs appear to refrain from involvement in activities relating to their agencies when it comes to public policy-making processes. Traditionally, chiefs have confined themselves to the execution of policies that evolve from the political process, denying appropriate input into many matters in which the police service has a special concern and obvious expertise. Communities are then robbed of valuable information necessary for the decision-making process which, of course, is controlled by politicians. Many agencies suffer the classical aftereffects of having political forces pass along problems they are either not properly suited to handle or which they cannot handle under the guidelines given to them. This makes a police agency appear to be the solution instead of a part of the problem-solving process. The cycle also is the leading cause of the police agency being reactionary, capable of responding to problems but not resolving them efficiently.

Police chiefs who only address administrative situations also appear to be the leaders who do not maintain a sense of their community. They are often found to have little influence in their communities, and their views are rarely known outside their departments. Even their officers become uncertain as to exactly what the chief stands for, creating further uncertainty of direction for the entire agency. Upper echelon leaders, in addition to the chief, should be spokespersons for the organization, and they must be able to relate and openly communicate with other leaders in their community. As Whitham's studies have shown, the development of relationships of trust and respect facilitate the accomplishments of an agency's purpose, and it can do so without usurping the electoral authority of politicians. Actually, the concept may strengthen the positions of politicians who encourage their department's upper echelon people to participate and openly develop relationships with other community leaders. This action, when employed with common sense and the proper protocols, enhances the quality of government performance from several perspectives.

Political Appointments

Political appointments are not likely to be abolished anytime soon in the law enforcement field, but planners can effectively support nationwide efforts to standardize qualifications and minimum requirements. Most politicians are acutely aware of the need to support police service movement toward professionalization. They can have the most impact if reforms are presented and accepted now with adherence to recommendations that were first proposed in the late 1970s and early 1980s. Planners should call upon research available from the International Association of Chiefs of Police (IACP), the Police Executive Research Forum (PERF), International City Managers Association (ICMA), and other public administration associations to formulate their proposals on essential minimum standards for top leaders of police departments. Some studies conducted by these organizations have provided information about the necessity of establishing standards in a form suitable for future considerations.

Although it is not necessary for top leaders to have served as police officers at all, it certainly helps. Those who are selected to lead a law enforcement agency without police and police management experience at various levels may find that their true understanding of the nature and capabilities of police service may be lacking. While these types of leaders do bring potentially fresh, unbiased approaches to police service, they also bring an untried and untested entity which often fails to gain quick acceptance in the closed circles of police work. Considering that the average tenure of a police chief is around four years, the noncareer leaders' hopes lie in a strong staff, an open reception from the rank-and-file, and no major crisis to deal with before they can establish their program. It has been done, but rarely. In the future, police service may be more prepared to accept this type of leader, but not until old traditions and interisolatory politics lessen their grips.

Another distasteful ingredient which often accompanies noncareer appointees is their conspicuous appearance as patronage minions. Regardless of their backgrounds or educational level, most are proceeded by a stereotyped image which will continue to loom in police organizations for some time to come. The organization usually does not fully accept this type of person's leadership, because they will be replaced when another political administration comes into power. A honeymoon period exists for this type of leader, but the career law enforcement manager still offers the most promising alternative.

BASES FOR COMPENSATION

Of all the traditions and similarities which bind the 10,000 police agencies in this country, insufficient financial compensation leads the list. One major reason for this continuing problem is that there has never been an effective way to gauge the cost of policing; therefore, no effective method of determining the actual level of financial rewards which should accompany the work have ever been agreed upon by governing bodies. Police administrators have argued in the past that the work is dangerous and stressful. By using the spin-off contentions that often accompany those facts, administrators have simply relied upon emotional pleas to unsympathetic budget brokers to improve police pay. It's been a hit-and-miss process. Sometimes it works, but more often than not it only increases the frustrations for the police seeking pay increases. Since society does not yet see police work or law enforcement as a profession, compensation increases have been negligible.

Adverse Reactions from Police Service Center

Although corruption issues are quick to get the attention of the public, thus forcing politicians and those who approve budgets to plan for pay increases, the argument that police service deserves more pay to avoid corruption is a worthy but weak debate. The 1970s saw a rise in the number of police agencies seeking unionization or collective bargaining rights. Contrary to public belief, this was not the first time this century that the service witnessed police officers who were willing to strike for higher pay. In 1889, the New York Police Department walked out when pay was reduced, but Boston's police strike of 1919 will be remembered most because rioting broke out and people were killed in that city during the strike. These events laid the groundwork for staunch opposition to police unionization. Communities and politicians feared that a unionized police corp would result in deterioration of the public interest and possibly spur sympathy strikes by police for other union brotherhoods, causing additional problems for government. Many people felt, and still do, that police officers who were hired to protect the public simply could not be given the right to strike, leaving a community without police deterrent.

Continued frustrations and the success of other unionized groups encouraged the police service to push even harder for higher wages through collective bargaining. In 1959, Wisconsin was the first state to grant this right to police officers. Soon the country was experiencing a wave of collective bargaining petitioners from police service. There will continue to be both positive and negative arguments about police unionization; but without question, the failure to deal with police compensation issues can be attributed to the long list of failures associated with police management. The failure to effectively bring about the change in attitudes about police service and police officers necessary to convince government to deal with police compensation will remain on the shoulders of the police administrators from the early and mid-point of this century.

The Cost of Policing

In the struggle to identify an effective cost of policing, some administrators depend on the formula of measuring police officers required to police by **officers per thousand**. This formula suggests that a cost of policing can be calculated if an agency knows how many officers it will take to handle crimes reported or experienced in a community. Some administrators justify their department strength allotment in the same fashion, but the formula does not reflect the true costs of policing. There have been other situations where an administrator determines the size and budget of an agency on the comparison of size and budget of another agency which polices another city of similar size in another state. This type of management and the results of this type of **research** upon which to make decisions also fails to hold water. Planners must start considering ways to convince officials that even though police salary budgets may be a lion's share of the overall police budget (usually about 90 percent), a truer cost of policing a community must be found. Once a more accurate accounting is possible, a more meaningful definition of what police officers should be paid will follow.

Few citizens will disagree that police deserve higher wages, but few will agree on exactly how much of a higher wage is deserved. No one wants to pay more taxes voluntarily, so planners need a good grasp of making every dollar spent worth the effort. This concept extends most importantly in the area of adequate compensation standards for police officers. Since there is no unified or validated formula to gauge the actual cost of policing in this country, planners should be prepared to work towards more equitable pay classifications in the 1990s. Through a sound compensation plan that not only appropriates sufficient wages for police but includes incentives for officers pursuing specialization or advancing into management, planners may be able to use their future budgets more intelligently and more effectively. Using budgets to more adequately promote for fundamental financial needs of officers can result in a finely-tuned management corp and more effective police officers for the 1990s and beyond.

This use can also quickly advance the development of law enforcement's potential managers while supplementing the progression for more effective police officers by adequately compensating for both responsibility levels and career development.

Police service pay systems can be directly attributed to poor leadership and management practices. A system that requires promotional advances for an employee to increase wages is organizationally unhealthy. Some specialized assignments which increase an officer's pay because of hazardous duty or specialist pay supplements exist, but often these supplements are lost should an officer return to regular duties. However, the most damaging aspect of this pay system comes from the problem of having to promote people in order to raise their pay. Planners should look around their respective departments and see how many officers in leadership positions are in over their heads, primarily because they competed for advancement in order to get the pay increase. Most of the time, officers motivated for this reason alone are found to be not only ineffective leaders, but unhappy ones; because they, too, realize they left an area they enjoyed just for compensation enhancement. These types of leaders continue to advance into higher management ranks for the same reason as their careers continue. The end result can be devastating to the growth of modern management in police service. Few of these leaders ever develop the skills required to do more than merely serve in some position to which they have been promoted. They are a group who would rather be supervised and led by others; however, once ego and intermittent sparks of ambition come into play, their positions are usually used to exercise their formal powers, another throwback to autocracy. There are periodic pay step increases for police officers in most police departments, but the increases are not commensurate with duties or responsibilities, and the system often pays everyone practically the same amount even when some officers have more work and more responsibility. In terms of planning a career in law enforcement, an officer has to consider competing for rank in order to financially advance.

This problem has a reverse impact on officers in police service who have a desire to develop into managers. The size of the agency may dictate fewer ranking slots. Fewer slots mean less opportunity for advancement; and when there are officers who are more adept at taking promotional exams, the officers who have a genuine desire to develop themselves as leaders may not have the chance to get started. Planners can certainly understand the loss of motivation experienced by officers in those positions. The existence of this system further solidifies officers' beliefs that individual talents, skills, and contributions to the agency are taken for granted by administrators who **recognize** only officers who are promoted.

Compensation Planning that Makes Sense

Pay systems in law enforcement have also been a cause of fluctuating retention rates experienced since the 1970s. On the average, a well-trained officer with five years of experience represents an investment of around $100,000 for a governing body. Should an officer leave an agency because of the lack of financial opportunities, then police departments and communities lose. Another $100,000 must be found somewhere in the budget, and unfortunately there is no assurance that the same thing won't happen in another five years or less.

Most local and state governments do not distinguish between salary scales of police officers and other employees. The traditional step increases, based on time in the position and longevity pay along with cost of living increases, are usually all clumped together in standardized classifications.

A distinct and separate pay classification system is required for law enforcement. Planners need to isolate their organizations from the other entities of local and state government by developing a more creative system through which to adequately compensate as well as advance overall police service.

As previously discussed, recent studies show that wages are not a priority concern for modern workers, but planners need to take into consideration other advantages for police service that arise from adequate compensation programs. As law enforcement slowly moves toward true professionalism, the balance of intrinsic and extrinsic rewards that will lure well-credentialed personnel into, and maintain them as a part of, the police service will become more critical. When the balance exists, more **professionals** will be motivated toward even higher performance standards, and the agency will maintain higher levels of conduct, discipline, efficiency, and morale.[37] A minimum entry level salary and a police salary structure separate and distinct from other government agencies will produce this result.

Career Ladders

Managerial and nonmanagerial career paths also should be developed in this separate structure. This approach, known in some progressive agencies as horizontal and vertical career ladders, will go far in preventing unsuitable leaders from emerging in police administration in the next century. The approach will also provide a higher probability that self-actualization will come sooner to officers following a vertical path and lead to a more content police corp surfacing in an era when job satisfaction is essential for organizational advancement.

The nonmanagerial career path starts with the uniform patrol officer. Incentives from this path would allow a uniformed officer to advance in salary as the officer takes on more nonmanagerial studies or responsibilities within the uniformed patrol assignment. Ultimately, the goal of the program is to allow an officer who is competent and content in the duties of a uniformed patrol officer to remain in that assignment, but still advance to a salary level equal to or higher than that of a supervisor or specialist, like an investigator.

The managerial career path starts as soon as the officer is promoted to the first recognized level of supervisory responsibility within a department. That path must also incorporate progressive career steps built upon the need to complete certain educational and training levels, as well as experience and management skill development. This path should extend all the way to the command staff.

Merit principles come into play during the planning of this type of system. Merit principles often conflict with civil service regulations, so this career path concept must be governed without regulations which inhibit the flexibility of the concept. This fact usually draws the most criticism from governing bodies because of the sacredness of civil service standards. Planners must be prepared to convince opponents that civil service standards have demanded only mediocrity from police officers and that these standards must be more flexible to incorporating career path concepts. Civilians employed by police agencies must have programs within this concept as well.

Compensation is a complex problem for police. Larger cities such as Los Angeles have long ago adopted career path programs which work well for an agency that size. Small and some mid-sized departments will have a tougher time convincing their governing bodies to adopt a progressive career path plan; but in order for law enforcement to improve as a service across the country, this type of compensation classification system is necessary. Governments have to divorce themselves from the shallow philosophy that increases must be given across the board whenever they are given. The continuance of this practice only digresses from and prevents other needed advancements in police management and organizational development.

INTERAGENCY POLITICS

It may be debated whether interagency or office politics should be included in a road map for practitioners, but planners who know their business realize that this broad form of unofficial manipulation has devastated more often than it has benefited police management. The frustrations that arise as a result of office politics thwart efficient planning efforts. The rejection of imaginative and creative programs as a result of interagency politics only enriches the gamesman's position and causes setbacks which stunt organizational growth altogether. Office politics is all about survival and knowing what could happen before it happens. Most of the time, office politics centers around the concept that one may either encourage or prevent something from happening which will help or hurt personally. Practically every manager has played the game to a certain degree. Those who haven't are probably recently promoted.

Basic Strategies Used by the Interagency Politician

Most office politicians may be suitably described as weak and insecure. Some engage in the practice because of impatience or perhaps because they have not yet learned the destruction that lingers in the wake of politicking. The Research Institute of America determined from a study in the mid-1980s that the higher up the ladder, the more managers demonstrated a tendency toward openness as well as on-the-record dealing. At the lower end of the management scale and with younger managers, there was marked tendency to feel that subterfuge, deviousness, and strategy were essential to getting ahead.[38] Chronic games will enjoy limited success if upper management is less tolerant of this practice, but that apparently only stands true in theory. There are essentially six categories of basic strategies used by the interagency politicians. The actual design or form of the maneuverings, of course, varies with the personalities and the circumstances:

1. **PLAYING IT SAFE:** One of the major charges against the politically adept is that they never commit themselves to any particular program or plan of action until they are certain which way the wind is blowing. This overeager individual is pictured as having two major aims: ... to be noticed by the right people; and ... to keep his own record clean. This avoidance of risk is a potentially fatal defect. Optimistic risk-taking is one of the foundations of leadership. Playing it safe only stunts initiative.

2. **BACK-BITING:** The most **advanced** politician turns his energies toward narrowing the field of competition. Results come in a variety of ways, ranging from planting of information in the right places to the outright manipulation of facts. Gossip is common and rumors or some form of word-of-mouth is utilized. A light coating of humor may camouflage the actual attacks. When this type has the ear of a top manager, the information passed along is usually hand-picked and the encounters are rarely used for any purpose but to advance self interest.

3. **SWORDSMANSHIP WITH A PEN:** A couple of easily identifiable techniques are observed in this category. The gamesman com-

posing attention-getting memorandums, letters, and other **reports** usually does so in order to carbon copy politically important people. Other compositions are created for the record when this person suspects that the superiors may be treading on dangerous ground. Unwilling to risk a showdown by direct confrontation, he can at least minimize his own involvement by a carefully prepared statement addressed to the proper parties.

4. **STRATEGY AT MEETINGS:** The basic rule used by tacticians in this category is to not offend the brass. Nothing is more stunning to a person than to expose his actual weakness on a particular project or assignment in an open meeting. Therefore, in this situation, the gamesman will say nothing at all. Phony meetings often result, and no free exchanges of ideas take place. This coyness can be dealt with by calling meetings which include these types only when new ideas are the topic of the meeting.

5. **LINING UP A TEAM:** One of the symptoms of an advanced case of politics is excessive concern with the balance of strength. The skillful politician carefully musters the necessary strength in his own camp, but often plants seeds of his own demise. The **right amount** of strength is hard to measure; sometimes an ally takes control. In lining up colleagues to support an idea or project, the politically-minded will go after those who carry the most weight. However, overqualified or ambitious associates are rarely included because they are seen as a threat. Some indicators of this type of activity can be identified when tacticians begin to play associates one off against another; making sure the higher-ups are aware of the smallest errors made by those who are perceived as **threats;** side-tracking competitors' productivity by involving them in duplicate projects; taking others' credit as their own; and recommending for transfer those whose strength represents a threat. One way to offset this game is to make it clear to each leader that failure to develop competent assistants will result in heavy demerital ratings on performance appraisals and advanced assignment considerations.

6. **THE FREEZE-OUT:** Upper management has different techniques at their disposal. Those closer to the top are capable of swiftly damaging growth and advancement. In the lower ranks, a freeze-out can take place with ordinary bypassing. In the upper circles, a variety of more cruelly efficient ways have been developed for

elbowing a person out of the way. Most are calculated to frustrate the victim into just giving up. Some include:

... **forgetting** to notify the victim of conferences or meetings;

... **forgetting** to answer the victim's memos or phone calls;

... reassigning the victim to an unsuitable job;

... calling in an additional assistant; and

... bringing in another authority or creating a special committee to deal with a matter to make it appear that the victim is incompetent to handle parts of a task or job.

Five Principles of Destructive Political Activity

There is no single solution to the complex problem of office politics. Organizations are miniature societies. They produce disagreements over goals, methods, values, and distribution of rewards. Politics naturally emerge as a means for resolving such disagreements. Disruptive politics is another matter. Individuals who are predisposed to intrigue exist in all police organizations and other types of settings. They generally become important only when the structure of an organization encourages it. Political trouble, then, is part and parcel of the organizational blueprint and road map for the 1990s.

There are five principle causes that give rise to destructive political activity:

1. indefinite lines of responsibility;
2. uncertain criteria for advancement;
3. faulty communications;
4. overemphasis on group decision-making; and
5. interdepartmental competition.

Curbing Political Practitioners

When office politics emerges in virulent form, competition has broken the bonds of normalcy. It is the responsibility of planners to curb this internal problem and stop it in its tracks. Some methods to consider in launching assaults are:

• Stop bypassers as soon as they start. Do not permit **end runs**. Require that this person take up problems initially with the person involved.

• Press for facts. Nothing nonpluses a back-stabber as much as a

request for details. Idea-stealers, in particular, are easily nailed by
this technique.

- Set an example . . . and avoid becoming an amateur psychoanalyst
  when trying to figure out what elements in a person's personality
  makes him play politics. Stay in touch with the framework of the
  organization and focus attention on what can be done to correct
  organizational deficiencies that cause office politics.[39]*

COMMUNITY POLICING: A MATURE VISION

The various definitions of community policing which exist around
the country may suggest that this is just another trendy approach destined to fall short of its promise. The idea is hardly a new one. Vollmer's
criminologist concept for police was a forerunner of the community
policing principles seen today. Arthur Woods, New York City's Police
Commissioner during the second decade of this century, was another
strong supporter of the theme upon which community policing is based.
Community policing did not get off the drawing board in those times
because of the obstacles to reform, ranging from political corruption to
outright suppression of the concept by government leaders. The earliest
versions of community policing were centered around the contention
that police officers should be more socially-oriented and enlist community assistance to deter crime. The early supporters of these ideas are
now seen as too innovative for their times. It has taken more than half a
century for police to again look at the communities they serve as partners,
moving away from the stagnation associated with being merely a **response**
agency.

A planner may find several theoretical definitions of community
policing and how it is to neatly fit into police service. In reality, law
enforcement finds itself again in an infant stage of development in
community policing, and planners must analyze other agencies' community policing programs to see which approaches and styles would actually work in their respective areas. At this time, there is no clarity nor
uniformity in this type of program, but that may be the very element
which makes community policing so promising. A fundamental understanding of what this type of program can do serves as just enough

---

*The preceding material was reprinted with permission by the National Institute of Business Management,
Inc., N.Y.

impetus for planners to outline a workable program in their area. Differences in communities prevent programs that may work in one city from functioning at all in another. How the program is designed with a particular community's problems in mind may be the key to the development of community policing, converting rhetoric into reality.

There appear to be four programmatic components which serve as the foundation for developing community policing. These components are acceptable in theory and application as long as planners agree that the purpose of community policing is to involve the public in its own defense and to share the burden of protection with the police.[40] More complex definitions and expansions in theory exist, but planners who begin with this fundamental understanding of community policing can revise and possibly identify workable basics to improve the concept in the next decade.

Components of Community Policing

Community Crime Prevention

This element is the centerpiece. The principal elements of the Neighborhood Watch programs first developed in the 1970s still serve. Public surveillance, property marking, and home security must be incorporated in the overall design of any programs which enlist the community. In this design, neighborhoods develop the sense of the identity needed for individuals to pull together and share some of the responsibility for the safety of their neighbors and security of their property. It appears that the closer the police agency works with these types of neighborhood associations—the more interaction that exists—the more successful the program, and the more willing the community is to become extensively involved in the advancement of the concept.

Reorientation of Patrol Activities

One of the simplest to understand, this element also is the one that breaks tradition and is often subject to harsh disagreement. It forces managers to examine the ineffective way uniform patrol strategies are commonly used. The standard practice of the use of patrol officers to only **respond** to calls for service, instead of becoming more entrenched in the affairs of their communities, has to be rethought. Motorized patrol and communications technology have their place and always will in police service, but a total dependence on this structure fails to allow officers to do much more than cope with the consequences of problems.[41] A redeployment of patrol officers to decentralized assignments within a community rounds out some of the requirements of the community policing blueprint.

Increased Police Accountability

Agencies reluctant to open themselves up for close examination by the public will have trouble accepting this element as well, but community policing must incorporate the process of creating new opportunities for the public to voice their concerns directly to police. This will automatically cause police agencies to pinpoint exactly what their communities think of them. Some of the responses will not be flattering.[42] Planners must realize, though, that in order to enlist public support and, most importantly, the public's cooperation, they must be prepared to listen to what the public will tell them, however unpleasant.[43] One-way communication from the police simply will not work in any version of community policing.

Decentralization of Command

Police agencies traditionally profess that they are operated under a central command with a common mission. That overall philosophy is sound, but the literal application of this philosophy is out-of-touch with modern policing. Different communities have different policing priorities and problems within their boundaries, and obviously distinct differences exist between cities and states. Managers must be given the latitude and authority from their centralized command staff to act according to their own reading of respective local conditions.[44] This is especially true for state police organizations which may have as many as 20 different posts spread across a state, each with independent crime and community problems that cannot be effectively addressed through standardized strategies designed by a headquarters' staff. This decentralization must be present if police agencies are going to take full advantage of the **particular knowledge** that stems from the community policing approach and feedback from it.[45] The concept of substations, precincts, and sector houses has to be expanded to allow this latitude to fully blossom. Decentralization also demands and transforms the responsibilities of patrol officers and the mid-level management ranks, paving the way for a more self-directing officer to emerge.[46]

The Benefits of Community Policing for Police Service

Any planner should immediately grasp that community policing does not alter the essential objectives of law enforcement. What must be altered is the way administrators allocate police resources in order to adapt to emerging needs.[47] The one issue which may be a shining pathway on the road map, the community policing concept, is the most likely to facilitate the underlying but distant quest for police service to become more professionalized. Other benefits will also accrue when community policing is instituted in a response fashioned for the individual community.

Public Understanding and Confidence

By including the community in the efforts formerly handled by the police service alone, an improved understanding of the complexities surrounding police work will begin to shape public attitudes. A community which views itself as being in partnership with law enforcement will be more supportive. A lesser degree of resistance for program expansion should follow as the community asks its elected officials to do more to support programs which advance law enforcement.

Increased Police Morale

As contacts with the community multiply through community policing measures, police officers begin to see that there is support for law enforcement, support which up to this point has been rarely seen or demonstrated by a community. The traditional deployment of officers results in the police being in contact with the worst elements of society. Community policing extends to police an opportunity to deal with other groups, offering a side of society too rarely witnessed by police—the citizens who welcome their presence.[48] This freshness is not only a morale booster, but a new viewpoint for police officers who have become used to the isolation of their patrol cars and a relief from the stress associated with dispatches to emergency situations.

Satisfaction

The more responsibility an officer is given, the more challenging the officer's assignment becomes. The components of community policing may not be completely suited to veterans who are stuck on tradition. It may take the attitudes of a new generation to make the concept work. But as police service gets its share of a modern, more educated work force, planners may find that community policing provides those who are less accepting of routine with an incentive to become more creative and imaginative, and they will get more out of their careers. Those who do will certainly benefit police service into the next century.

ACCENTUATING COMMUNITY UNDERSTANDING

People are curious about police work. Television, books, and films ensure that many people who never come into contact with the criminal justice system harbor voyeurisms about police activities. Many of the images are wrong, giving rise to some absurd perceptions that police officers are more than just regular people. By looking inside these misconceptions, a planner can easily see that people who are confused about police officers are likely to be thoroughly confounded by the true complexities of police service and police organization.

Strangely enough, it is not just the television junkie who often shows signs of confusion about police work. People from all walks of life seem to have little accurate information about what it is like to be a police officer or to be a part of an organization bound by laws and regulations. Police officers have always understood that even their closest friends and relatives don't really understand, much less appreciate, the true make-up of service, how the work interrelates with society, and the underlying complications involved. Some of this leads to the development of closed circles, isolating officers and their work from the community. It certainly leads to diversified forms of fraternal bonding between officers, which may or may not be healthy for the organization or the officers.

A planner can break down this problem by manipulating the various ways in which the community is exposed to its police department. No police administrator wants his department to be gauged only by those upon whom enforcement actions are taken. Little community understanding is promoted by hoping that news stories about arrests or property recoveries will show how well the police are doing. Community service units can talk and make presentations all day long, every day of the year, and still fall short of truly making a community understand the intricacies of policing. There are many worthwhile and important programs involving the community in various ways; and those measures are important, each chipping away at misconceptions and accentuating community understanding. But planners should study alternatives which pull all of these efforts together and present service in its proper light, thus bringing about more community understanding while actually allowing the community to **witness** the work first-hand.

The need for community understanding should be obvious for planners who realize the role that the community must play in the future of law enforcement efforts. More groundwork needs to be laid at this time to facilitate and heighten understanding and awareness. The more that is accomplished in this area now, the less resistance will be experienced by police agencies in the future. An accentuated understanding can also lead to a fuller appreciation of the present tasks and those which lie ahead from not only the community in general, but from elected officials and other external sources of influence upon police organizations. This stop of the road map is simply an expansionary strategy to assist planners in rounding out their versions of community policing ideas and to provide the opportunity for the agency to promote its effectiveness to the community.

Some cities have developed brief seminars—one or two days—sponsored by their chambers of commerce. The seminars enlist persons from all levels of the community who may be considered future, or current, **community leaders.** The seminars organize classes and tours through government facilities which not only include the police department, but the court system and local correctional facilities. Representatives from each organization make a pitch on behalf of their organization, explain the purpose of their jobs, and give the participants an insider's view. Some programs go a step further by arranging for citizens to ride with police officers during their tours of duty or to **work** in their communications office. The programs generally get the point across, and few participants walk away with the same attitude toward police. The most common complaint heard from participants is that the program did not last long enough or that they would like to have had more time in certain areas (confirming the **natural curiosity** contention).

These people go back to their families, jobs, and community activities with their understanding of the police service in a different perspective. Certainly a lot of stereotypical and superficial imagery is broken down, perhaps meeting all the needs of some communities and police organizations. But, once again, this concept can be taken a step further by employing **community curiosity** to not only accentuate understanding, but to expose their officers and organization to a more positive atmosphere and progressive tone.

In 1987, the Commerce City, Colorado, Police Department expanded this concept and established a **Citizens' Police Academy.** This agency has around 50 full-time office and civilian employees to service a community with a daytime population of about 50,000. Their approach was bold; they asked citizens to attend a three-hour session once a week for eleven weeks. Optional activities took place on weekends. The Commerce City **academy** took participants through a course that ranged from firearms training to a review of civil liability issues faced by officers and police organizations.[49] The courses were not designed to make police reservists out of the citizens, but to simply elevate and intensify perceptions.

Applicants for this program were screened to assure that unsuitable or unstable people were prevented from becoming a disruptive influence, but no attempt was made to eliminate people who were nonsupportive of the agency or police service. The participants in the agency's first program were a cross-section of citizens, which enhanced the discussion periods and furthered the concept of the program. No special budgetary revisions were necessary to arrange this program. Speakers from within and outside the agency participated.

The Commerce City police found that lectures held little interest to the participants. Involvement in actual ride-along programs and going through the department's drive course and firing range were true catalysts which incited other interests. The small size of each class allowed such close monitoring and supervision during these types of sessions that liability issues and concerns were minimal.

The response the Commerce City police received from the program has called for other classes to be conducted. They are now ongoing. The department declares the program a success and have found an additional benefit in that their officers and managers now see the community in a different light as well. The perspective provides planners with a first-hand account of the concerns of people in their community.

This particular approach may not be the exact vehicle through which other agencies accentuate community understanding, but variations of the concept can improve citizen relations. Planners who capitalize on the public's inherent inquisitiveness about police officers and police work through this concept will pave a lot of the rough roads ahead.

MEASURING PRODUCTIVITY AND
THE REWARD STRUCTURE

Measuring the performance of police organizations has been a topic of debate for decades. Many agencies which proclaim to be progressive and in touch with the multiple changes in society are usually found to still rely heavily upon the traditional activity categories which do not accurately nor consistently reflect the true workload. Organizational performance of a police agency is extremely difficult to gauge when it is dominated by the systems and programs based upon outdated reward structures. The difficulty increases when elected officials rely on the 50-year-old Uniform Crime Report system to exclusively measure the direction and effectiveness of a community's police department. But, ultimately, fault must be placed on police managers who fail to devise a more equitable measuring stick for use by their planning staffs, elected officials, and the community.

By its very nature, service is a more difficult commodity to measure than a manufactured product. Service is often delivered only on request of the client, a factor over which the agency has little control. If the quantity cannot be measured, then the quality of the service will also be difficult to measure.[50]

It could be said that police organizations appear to have a fetish for the written word. Very little happens, administratively or criminally, that is not reduced to a document or, more often, many documents. This practice has ultimately led police agencies to be the official community **historian** and archivist, maintaining records and actions of the seamy side of life.[51] Measuring productivity through this means of documentation results in police organizations being gauged entirely upon their ability to record crimes in their archives.

Police service has always used the crime rate, the number of arrests, and cases cleared as the center of their productivity justifications and explanations. Heavy emphasis on these categories certainly represents information needed by planners and of interest to the public, but they are not and cannot be the basis of gauging a contemporary agency's productivity.

The Uniform Crime Report

The development of the Uniform Crime Report (UCR) system in 1930 by the IACP was the first nationwide crime information collection program devised and used in the United States. Participation in the program is voluntary, thus many agencies did not initially take part. Many sheriff's departments did not participate until after the mid-1960s; and without full participation of the various law enforcement agencies that dealt with reported crime, only a representative sample of information was available for analysis. Today, nearly 16,000 law enforcement agencies voluntarily contribute.

The UCR program was designed to gather information about reported crime, victims, arrests, suspects, and stolen property, as well as other data vital in examining even the demographics of crime. The FBI was authorized by Congress to serve as a clearinghouse for statistical information reported under criteria formulated by UCR. Categorized information, reported monthly from participating police agencies, serves as the basis of the data bank, and from this data the public learns of the increases and occasional decreases of reported crime on the 6 o'clock network news several times a year. The release of information is heralded by some police administrators as the means through which they may tout their organization's effectiveness or explain why their agency may be experiencing difficulty in coping with increases. The figures represent the national crime picture, and reporting agencies are also provided and fed back information about local crime rates. The primary categories of crimes used in this analysis are the Part I crimes. The UCR program declared in 1930 that these were the crimes which were most serious and took place most frequently, as established by studies across the nation in the late 1920s. These Part I crimes were identified as murder, forcible rape, robbery, aggravated assault, burglary, larceny-theft, and motor vehicle theft. Due to the rising number of reported arsons, that crime was added to this category in 1979. This group of offenses is most commonly referred to and known as the Crime Index.

Early in the UCR's planning, it was recognized that the differences among criminal codes used in various states precluded a mere aggregation of state statistics to arrive at a national statistic. Variances in punishment for the same offense in different states prevented even basic distinctions between felony and misdemeanor crimes. To avoid the problems and to provide nationwide uniformity in crime reporting, standardized offense definitions were formulated. Today, agencies submit data in accordance to UCR definitions without regard for local statutes.

The True Worth of the Crime Index as a Measurement

The UCR system has remained virtually unchanged since 1930. In the early 1980s, a national review of the system resulted in some revisions of the definitions used to classify Part I crimes. The FBI used a pilot program with these revisions in 1985 in one state to determine if a nationwide application of the new process would work.

UCR has served an important role in criminal justice. Reporting guidelines are rigid and the data collected is about as good as it is going to get for the nation and maybe for most states. States reporting to UCR have to meet certain conditions, and their data must guarantee consistency and comparability. These conditions result in what is often thought to be the first nationalization action seen in this country. This uniformity may be improved upon as time passes, but UCR presents other problems for police service. The absence of other methods to measure reported crime and to gauge police organization effectiveness has often elevated these crime stats to a level of importance that may go far beyond their actual worth. Some authorities have argued that the methodology of collection and the numerous interpretations of definitions may affect the reported Crime Index more than anything the police may actually do in response. The UCR's existence also implies to some police administrators and elected officials that their state and local agencies do not need to undertake any other collection of data which may more accurately measure their performance on the state and local level. The UCR system does not prohibit agencies from gathering **other statistical data** beyond the national collection. It is this **other statistical data** which can prove vital to police planning and community understanding of the true effectiveness of their agency and the totality of their workload.

One of the best examples of this need to collect, analyze, and publicize **other statistical data** can be found by examining the UCR's classification of drug offenses. As this time keen community interest focuses on the issues surrounding drug availability and enforcement. Agencies must collect appropriate data which in some terms measures the availability of illicit drugs in the community, removals, reporting, case work and other critical areas which assist planners in measuring their enforcement strategies. When UCR reports are made public and scrutinized by the media and elected officials, there is no information about the scope or influence of drug availability included. Communities are not made aware of the strides, or lack thereof, by their police department. And most public officials, unless they inquire, do not automatically see the influences of workloads in their area. Drug offenses are Part II crimes under the UCR and are not part of the widely used Crime Index. Whenever the Crime Index is used, it should be backed up with supplemental information which reflects other areas of law enforcement responsibilities in order to portray a more accurate picture of the problems in the community.

The Inclusion of a Nonenforcement Gauge

Often community and elected officials are not congnizant of the true purpose behind the UCR. Planners must include in their blueprints a method to indoctrinate both officials and the community. If the Crime Index is used literally, police organizations should theoretically only dedicate their resources to the Part I crimes. As community policing and other broad law enforcement concepts are instituted, the true value of using the Crime Index will come into focus. However, planners are already in a position to redesign the foundation of productivity measurements; more creative approaches need to be developed. The nonenforcement and service-related categories need to be incorporated into a comprehensive stick alongside arrests and property recovered. The emphasis on areas declared most important will necessitate a shift in conventional administrative philosophy. The public must be exposed to the vast number of duties for which their police agencies are responsible. The amount of time and effort required to handle the volume of administrative and support tasks needs to be included in order to reflect the overall complexities of the task. This can lead to an improved understanding of the organization's limits as well as its abilities.

This approach leads to a new reward structure for police officers. Motivated through this redesigned structure, officers will be recognized for services in addition to enforcement actions. The process will lend itself to the emphasis required from future managers to direct and encourage more officer involvement in the community on a scale compatible with future demands from society on police service.

OFFICER HEALTH, STRESS, AND COST EFFECTIVENESS

Each police officer represents a tremendous financial investment for state and local governments. Practically every law enforcement agency has some entry level fitness testing of candidates, but few have after-hiring physical fitness maintenance programs. Police service has been slow to recognize the value to these types of programs despite overwhelming evidence that police officers suffer an enormous amount of stress and physical deterioration from their work. Officer survival concepts need to be translated into **career survival** concepts, and planners must research and establish sound programs reflecting the service's concerns for the well being of their workers, regardless of their position or assignment, from the day they are hired until the day they retire. Higher survival rates will follow. An improved physical condition of officers will lessen the influences of the stresses most often associated with police work. Of course, government costs related to the crippling effects will decrease. Officers will certainly benefit personally, but will also experience the necessary assurance that their organization is taking that extra step to care for them. The true beneficiary of after-hiring programs is the community. Improved mental attitudes resulting from such programs create a more positive attitude despite stressful conditions.

The Financial Investment in Police Officers and Career Survival

Planners may simply view this area in terms not related to cost-effective ideals. Can officers who are not physically fit perform their duties properly? Can officers with debilitating physical problems, like obesity, perform their duties under the rigors associated with street assignments? Common sense tells us the answers to these two questions; essentially, these facts should force planners to realize the necessity of after-hiring programs. Figures reviewed from validated studies across the country on this topic also underscore the problem. Officers are aggravated by hypertension, high cholesterol, heavy drinking, overweight, heavy smoking, and lack of sufficient exercise. Most alarmingly, the percentages in these categories may fluctuate from 15 percent to 13 percent of the entire force, roughly translating into around 30 officers in a 100-officer police agency. Those 30 could be the ones answering dispatches and handling duties which demand a suitably fit officer. Unfortunately, many of those 30 officers may not even know they are at risk, and planners for the 1990s must understand how these conditions affect a person working in one of the most emotionally dangerous jobs in society.

Mandatory Program Principles

Planners must develop the types of physical fitness programs most equitable for their agencies and officers based upon the acceptance of two principles. These principles may go against the grain of the traditional-thinking manager who believes police work is not subject to the same unmerciful depreciations of workers in other organizations. The principles of a mandatory program force managers to admit that:

1. Officers who are out-of-shape share a higher probability of injury and/or illness than officers who are in reasonably good shape.
2. Physiologically stronger officers increase the chances that injury or illness may be less serious or easier to recover from.[52]

Actually, the principles speak for themselves, and a no-nonsense approach in justifying an agency's development of a fitness program should meet little resistance from other planners or upper echelon administrators. Resistance may come from officers who see a program of this nature as threatening in itself. After all, lifestyles have to be altered by those who are not fit. There is a change, not only in work-related habits but in off-duty habits and even family life which may be disrupted to a degree. How the program is introduced, as with any change management process, will offset some of the resistance a planner may encounter. Further research into this area will provide planners with information supporting the contention that this type of program is a necessity, and providing insights on how other agencies introduce their programs. Planners will also find that much of the anticipated resistance from those participating in the program will be erased by the officers' families who often see these programs as true life-saving measures.

Department size should make no difference to the planner. Facilities and expertise to help develop a fitness program can be located in practically every jurisdiction. There are costs associated with the development and operation of such programs, but planners are reminded that this is one area in which figures speak for themselves. The General Health Corporation estimated that the cost of a mid-level management employee suffering a heart attack is $60,000 in direct costs, such as lost productivity.[53]

Can cities and states afford such costs, especially when the costs are transfigured and multiplied to cover all levels of police officers, not just mid-level management?

Another issue for planners in the 1990s arises from the identification of the problem itself. Existing and future research into this area will provide abundant documentation to support the need for police organizations to establish these types of programs. Knowing the relationship between poor fitness levels and health habits, and not doing anything about it, may place police organizations in a libelous position from the standpoint of the officers, families of officers, and from situations that may arise out of actions taken or not taken by unsuitably physical or emotionally stable officers.

FISCAL PLANNING: NEW DIRECTIONS AND TACTICS

The budgetary process for police agencies requires that planners become tacticians. Severe consequences await those who fail to aggressively tackle the annual, unglamorous tasks involved in the detailed budgetary effort. Fiscal competition among other departments in government can be fierce, but the politics which accompany budget preparation can assist planners in forming effective coalitions with other units of government and can be used as a managerial tool.[54]

The size of an agency will dictate the planner's involvement in the budgetary process. Minimal input may be the rule in departments where there is no functional specialization and where the chief prepares the organization's funding request with little or no input from other managers.[55] A voice in budgetary requirements from managers at all levels is necessary. Even though each manager may not have his specific suggestions included, participation in the process can overcome the budget being prepared in isolation which can result in a chief administrator passing over certain funding considerations which may advance the agency.

Planners who are just now becoming familiar with the various types of budgetary planning may be overwhelmed with their surface complexity. The titles alone imply misunderstanding: line item budgets, performance budgets, programmatic budgets, planning program budgeting systems, zero-based budgets, hybrid budgets. Each serves a particularly useful purpose, and a little study can alleviate the misunderstanding

and the unwillingness of some managers to become more familiar with
the true value of long-range budget planning.

Fundamental Principles of Fiscal Planning

Sound fiscal planners need only understand the fundamental principles upon which most budgetary processes operate in order to expand
their skills in this area. Those fundamentals are:

- State and local governments have limited resources regardless of
  their tax base.
- There are always more worthwhile things to be done than are
  possible with the limited resources available to all state and local
  governments.
- A budget is an allocating device.

Harry More and John Kenney make these basic points in their **Police
Executive Handbook** text, but the most important fact a planner should
grasp on that topic is made clearer in the following passage:

> The police department has no vested right to a share of the resources.
> It must be able to demonstrate the need, the job to be done, in exact
> contrast to the almost infinite variety of things that could be done.[56]

Many police departments are awarded a lion's share of available
funds, but the majority of the budget is dedicated to the salaries of the
officers. Bottom line figures are misleading. An agency with a $5 million
budget may actually only have around 6 to 7 percent of that total budget
through which to fund the various other activities required or planned
for by the agency. The 1990s will not assure any excessive funds through
which to advance police service. Planners must find ways to ensure that
their organizations' progress can be effectively underwritten. Since the
police have little voice in tax bases, planners must do more to fully
justify their budget development.

The Inclusion of Agency Members in Fiscal Planning

City council persons or state legislators, no matter how qualified to
judge law enforcement and police service needs, must have facts on
which to base their budgetary decisions. Without them, their decisions
will not be uniformly sound, and appropriations could be based on
misconceptions, personal bias, individual acquaintances in and out of

the agency, and other extraneous factors.[57] In the absence of facts, planners should prepare to be disappointed from the unsympathetic response and the limited appropriations. A budget package must be fully justified, explained, and accompanied by substantiating facts which make council persons, legislators, and government administrators see the necessity of the requests.

One of the best ways to accomplish this goal is by delegating the responsibility of final presentations to the people who are going to run the programs. While a chief or commander of the planning unit may be worthy orators, their efforts are seen as a requirement of their positions; they need the money because they want the program. Those who are going to run the program or those who originated the concept for the program may best explain and substantiate the reasons behind the need and how the increased budget will actually benefit the officer doing the work and, ultimately, the community. This approach involves officers. It makes the budget planning and development process a unique tool for managers through which various levels of police officers may be used to help get programs funded and into action. With the backing of the chief, the actual presentation may make the difference, and without question the interpretation of the presentation depends a great deal on the person making it. The process can be time-consuming, but preplanning can streamline the approach. Another benefit of this tool is the exposure this type of planning and presentation can give to those involved. A better understanding of priorities, the direction of the community, and fiscal conditions of the government will be experienced. Valuable experience will enhance the approaches to be used in future budget requests, as well as make officers and managers more aware of other problems in government which they must be more in touch with in order to be effective.

Utilizing personnel in this fashion will not only open up the agency so that officers feel more a part of the planning for the future, but will also open creative expressions, allowing managers to see the work of some people who might otherwise never have the opportunity to reveal a talent in this functional specialty.

External Funding Resources

Future planners must also view external funding sources available to police service. In addition to the Federal grants awarded through the United States Department of Justice, many private organizations as well as private industries offer grants-in-aid or funding on projects in areas of special interest. This assistance may come in the form of cash or it may come in the form of donated equipment such as computers. Identifying the sources in a specific community should be a priority. What may not be allocated in a budget may be available from one of these sources if the proper structures are in place for receiving them and assuring that the benefits go to the advancement of the agency, not an individual. Appropriations of this nature are not inherently wrong as some managers may think. In reality, the sources are in place in many instances for this very purpose. Planners who refuse to at least research similar programs in their areas are doing their agencies an injustice.

NATIONAL ACCREDITATION FOR POLICE SERVICE

Imagine for a moment that you were asked to create an outline, one that would be used by a new city to develop a new police department. Your outline is needed to organize the following:

- role and authority
- jurisdiction, mutual aid, regional services
- contractual agreements for police services
- relationships with other agencies
- organization, direction, general management
- fiscal management, allocations of personnel
- planning and research, crime analysis
- career development, high education
- collective bargaining
- recruitment, selection, training, promotion, evaluations
- operations, support services, traffic
- auxiliary and technical services (i.e., communications, records, property management)

A planner's dream, right? Being able to start from scratch and develop all the proper formulas for a modern workable program, to set the organizational stage which would permit a smoother evolution of the agency with synchronized efficiency in relation to changes that will take place in society over the next several years. Where would you start? Some research into how a few of the largest agencies operate would be a likely starting point, then to scale those agencies' programs to the level required for this new police department.

The Concept and Accreditation Commission

Coming up with all the components necessary to establish a police organization which would be capable of being closely associated with the characteristics of a profession is nothing that has not already been done by the Commission on Accreditation for Law Enforcement Agencies. The necessary standards have been identified since 1982, and it is amazing how many planners in the service fail to at least take advantage of their existence even if their agency chooses not to undergo an accreditation process. One reason many agencies have not adopted some of the standards or care to pursue accreditation is that the program is voluntary and often misunderstood.

By this time in the next century, planners will look back at the accreditation process and attribute a majority of the advancements made toward professionalism to this concept, now in its infant stage. It may even be libelously dangerous for police agencies not to pursue accreditation in the near future.

The program is a joint effort of the Commission and four major law enforcement executive membership associations:

- International Association of Chiefs of Police (IACP)
- National Organization of Black Law Enforcement Executives (NOBLE)
- National Sheriff's Association (NSA)
- Police Executive Research Forum (PERF)

The Commission was formed in 1979 to establish a body of standards designed to (1) increase agencies' capabilities to prevent and control crime, (2) increase effectiveness and efficiency in the delivery of services, (3) increase cooperation and coordination with other agencies, and (4) increase citizen and employee confidence in the goals, objectives, policies, and practices of agencies. In addition, the Commission was to develop an accreditation process that provides state and local law enforcement agencies the opportunity to demonstrate **voluntarily** that they meet an established set of widely accepted law enforcement standards.

The four associations joined to create the Commission, appointing member representatives from law enforcement agencies, public officials, and private sector business representatives. The Commission was incorporated by the four associations in 1980. Once standards had been selected, field testing of the standards were implemented in 1982 and 1983. The funding for the original development of this concept was through a grant from the Law Enforcement Assistance Administration (LEAA) in 1979.

Standards Development, Scope and the Applicability of the Standards

The Commission defined 48 topics to be addressed in the form of standards and approved recommendations from staffs and committees concerning the elements of the standards, such as commentaries explaining the standards' purpose and what level of compliance was required for an agency. A structured field review of these standards was tested by selected departments representing 50 states. Amendments and consolidations resulted, and by 1983 the Commission had identified and based the process on 944 standards.

The Commission's accreditation manual has 48 chapters which address standards broken into three parts: standard statement, commentary, and levels of compliance. The standard statement is declarative and places clear-cut requisites on an agency. Some call for the development and putting in place of a policy on procedure or other action. The commentary explains or expands upon the standard to provide further guidance which the agency may or may not see necessary to follow when complying with the standard. Only the requirements of the standard statements are binding; the commentaries are not. Compliance indicates whether a standard is mandatory. Some standards may be mandatory for agencies due to size, but are not applicable to smaller agencies. There is also a level of compliance rating given when a full compliance is not required, but when compliance in some form is necessary. Certain standards apply whether or not an agency performs the function. All agencies are expected, for example, to analyze and to engage in community relations and crime prevention efforts. The scope of these requirements are outlined in the standards.

Agencies undergoing accreditation are expected to comply with at least 80 percent of the applicable nonmandatory standards, and agencies are free to select the 80 percent with which they choose to comply. Over a course of time, agencies seeking reaccreditation are expected to exceed this 80 percent requirement.

The Process and Procedures for Accreditation

There are five steps in the accreditation process:

1. APPLICATION: The process begins when the agency applies to the Commission.
2. AGENCY QUESTIONNAIRE: The agency completes and files the profile of its organization, which is used by the Commission to determine the standards with which the agency must comply.
3. SELF–ASSESSMENT: The agency initiates the self-assessment process to see if it complies with all applicable standards. Proof of the compliance is then assembled and reviewed in the next step.
4. ON–SITE ASSESSMENT: After an agency is satisfied that it has reached compliance with all applicable standards, the Commission identifies a team of assessors, reviews the assessors with the agency to avoid conflicts of interest, and then sends the team to the agency. Assessors review the proof of compliance at the agency.
5. COMMISSION REVIEW: The on-site assessment team submits its findings to the Commission. The Commission then either grants full accreditation or defers the accreditation status. When an agency fails to achieve the status, the Commission advises the agency what steps are necessary to gain accreditation.

Accreditation is for a five-year period. Agencies must remain in compliance with those standards under which accreditation was awarded during this period. Reaccreditation must be applied for during the fifth year, and on-site assessment is required in order for an agency to be reaccredited.[58]

The Value of the Accreditation Tool

In 1988, there were 79 law enforcement agencies in the United States which were accredited by the Commission. These agencies range in size from 21 to 2,490 full-time personnel. Another seven await accreditation letters. Some 600 other agencies are in the process of being accredited, 290 of which are in the self-assessment stage. It usually takes from 18 months to two years for an agency to complete this process due to various factors. Agencies may have to plan budgets, equipment purchases, and some program development around the process in order to establish their proof of compliance to the on-site assessors. The quickest an agency has moved through the process is one year; the Connecticut State Police already had many of the mandatory standards in place which facilitated their accreditation process.

Considering the more than 16,000 law enforcement agencies in the United States, the vision of accrediting each may be more of an hallucination than a reality if viewed as a cure-all for the decentralization and diversity of police service in America. It is this very decentralization which allows local and state governments to differentiate the roles that their police agencies should play in communities around the country. Centralizing the role of law enforcement organizations is not the purpose of the Commission, nor the concept. Upgrading police effectiveness and advancing the characteristics of professionalism within law enforcement are.[59] Many current administrators are leery of accreditation and are concerned that the process may eventually **force** an agency to be accredited under the Commission's standards in order to defend itself against civil actions based on the absence of an accreditation status. Others fail to see the benefits of going through the process in order to upgrade their organization and correct long-term deficiencies. Attracting higher qualified recruits, justifying personnel policies, enhancing community support, advancing cooperative efforts within other components of the criminal justice system, and establishing the foundation of a well-greased organization machine seem to escape their logic. In essence, those who argue the most against the accreditation concept are those who know very little about it and have not bothered to look at the advantages gained by those agencies who have undergone the process in the past several years.

The process will not only enhance the police organization which may already meet the majority of the standards, but it will enable a struggling organization to **start again** to architecturally redesign its agency and bring it into a more contemporary format which can evolve more efficiently and in concert with change. The reaccreditation every five years will maintain this contention. Once accreditation is achieved by an agency, it seems doubtful that an agency would allow that status to lapse, especially in today's litigious society.

The cost of the accreditation process is based on the individual agency's number of sworn and civilian employees. For example, an agency with 500 to 999 employees would be classified as an E-2 agency by the Commission, and the cost of the accreditation process would be around $14,000. The reaccreditation process averages about the same.

There are critics of the accreditation process who seem overly concerned about the federal funding that has been used to research and develop this Commission. Since 1979, over $2 million has been appropriated to the effort from the LEAA and the Department of Justice. The Commission is, of course, charging a fee for the accreditation process which returns funds to the program, but in no way do the fees appear able to reach the stage of profit-making for the Commission. As the concept proves itself effective, the Commission is likely to reduce dependance on federal government fundings and seek other sources of revenue through which to continue their program. A move in this direction may lessen resistance since the appearance of being just another federal program still hangs over the Commission in some administrators' opinions.

Planners may choose to carefully study the standards and process and compare the standards against those already in place within their agency. Some may feel that their standards and operations are already better that those designated by the Commission, and that little may be accomplished by this additional undertaking.

Planners in this situation may reflect further on the marketing and integration of the blueprint currently being used by their agency. Is the blueprint being used to maximize and advance their agency internally or externally? Would a slight readjustment in some areas through an accreditation process strengthen their blueprint for the future? An honest appraisal will bring many planners to the point of subscribing to the accreditation concept. No matter how many times the island organization says it is **modernized, professional**, or **advanced**, nothing attests these proclamations but the agency itself. Attitudes and proclamations change, as do organizational leaders, managers, and elected officials. Using a blueprint which is currently recognized as excellent, the **modernized** agency may actually lack the determined self-criticism necessary to pull itself beyond the inflated self-worth stature from which many isolated organizations suffer. A recognized accreditation process projects balance, a balance immediately acceptable and usually encouraged by communities that want to hear that what their officials have been telling them is backed up and that their police department is, by modern standards, accredited.

A revolutionary aspect of the accreditation process is that the public does have a say during the on-site assessment, and this participative role further enhances the service. Public credibility can heighten after an accreditation process, and planners may enjoy a parallel increase in their department's morale and pride. Planning for the future will, in itself, meet less resistance, and an agency's community support will be cast in a slightly different mold, further enhancing the organization's effectiveness. It will take time, and those still looking for immediate gratification will be disappointed if they continue seeking overnight turnarounds.

The accreditation of law enforcement agencies on a national basis is not a move toward a nationalized police corp; it is a move toward professionalism and a solid standardization of practices through which police service can efficiently evolve well into the 21st century. Accreditation provides a clear route on this road map for officers, managers, politicians and, most importantly, the citizens of the communities which are served.

THE ECHOING EFFECTS OF SOCIETY'S ATTITUDES

Planners who have listened carefully to the echoes of society's changing attitudes about crime over the past 20 years will agree that crime is viewed as less acceptable. That attitude accelerates change across the nation. Forecasts and predictions suggest trends and crimewarps which may influence and affect the nation's way of life, but it is the **community's attitude** toward crime that will determine acceptable levels. As taught by scholars in the past, crime will expand according to our willingness to put up with it, and that willingness appears to be decreasing as the 1990s approach.

Through the Crime Index mechanism of analyzing reported crime, a nation was informed that crime was decreasing in the 1980s. The decrease lasted until around 1985, when FBI Director William H. Webster, while noting a slight increase in the last quarter of 1984, announced that fewer crimes had been reported to law enforcement agencies than in any year since 1978.[60] Insightful authorities recognized that the **trend** was coming to an end and that increases in reported crime could be expected. Speculation mounted as to the reasons behind the several-year decrease, and it was suggested by Dr. Steven R. Schlesinger, the head of the Bureau of Statistics which conducts national crime surveys, that the media may have attributed too much credit to the maturation of the baby boomers for the post World War II era.[61] Demographics may influence the Crime Index, but Schlesinger was correct in his admonishment that too much credit was being given to this single factor by anyone.

Factors Affecting the Crime Rate

Three criminal justice factors are more likely to influence the Crime Index than anything else. Schlesinger took the position that these factors primarily influence property crimes; but plainly, practitioners can see that the factors influence all criminal offenders. Those factors are:

1. the clearance rate (or the fear of being caught);
2. the probability of incarceration (or the chances of going to prison if caught); and
3. the incapacitative effect of imprisonment (or the more criminals that go to prison, the fewer who are in society to commit crime).[62]

The police may directly affect Factor 1, but they have only marginal control over Factors 2 and 3. While the police must provide evidence against criminal suspects which may lead to conviction, they cannot be held totally accountable for assuring that suspects are incarcerated when convicted or that prosecutors will zealously pursue convictions on offenses charged in lieu of plea bargaining or other liabilities present in that area of the system.

Statistically, Uniform Crime Reports show that when clearance rates are low, the crime rate increases, and vice versa. The UCR also bears out the contention that when the odds of going to jail for a crime go down, like in the 1960s, crime begins to increase. As the odds increase, like in the 1970s and 1980s, crime decreases.[63] In the mid-1980s, there were fewer crime victims and an increase in the nation's prisons of more than 170,000 inmates.[64]

The record reflects that there is a tangible connection. There are many variables influencing each of these criminal justice factors, and none can stand alone when planners are examining the areas in relation to their respective communities. But much of the underlying causes go back to community attitudes and their willingness to put up with crime.

The Impact of Society's Attitudes About Crime and Police

Statistical data has always enjoyed a dubious reputation; and when it comes to tallying crime rates, the entire system may be questioned when an error is discovered in the collection methods or presentation of that data. Planners should look at their own communities and compare the attitudes with the statistical data. Less permissive attitudes toward crime exist in communities with well-organized, police-supported neighborhood watch programs. This attitude exists in communities where private organizations assist the system and lobby for stiffer penalties and more strict enforcement of existing laws. Communities displaying this attitude usually see their judges impose harsher sentences; and statistical data, if correct, reflects these variances. Communities without this attitude present long-range problems for their police agencies; planners will have a difficult time corresponding their agency's enforcement direction with attitudes mirrored by the community.

The distillation of this understanding brings forth the **"We're mad as hell and we won't take it anymore"** posture that demands police organizations synoptically plan their enforcement direction in harmony with the attitudes of the communities they serve. Communities failing to grasp these factors which influence crime rates must be better informed by their police departments and other components of the criminal justice system in order for many of the outlines in the road map to be of meaningful consequence for practitioners in the 1990s.

ENDNOTES

1. Hunsaker, Phillip L., Alessandra, Anthony J., *The Art of Managing People*, N.Y., Simon and Schuster, 1986, p. 72.
2. Baker, Mark, *Cops*, N.Y., Simon and Schuster, 1985, p. 96.
3. Kelly, Patricia, *Police and the Media*, Bridging Troubled Waters, Springfield, Thomas, 1987, xiii.
4. Germann, A.C., Day, Frank D., Gallati, Robert R., *Introduction to Law Enforcement*, Springfield, Thomas, 1968, pp. 60–68.
5. Kelly, Patricia, *Police and the Media*, Bridging Troubled Waters, Springfield, Thomas, 1987, p. 193.
6. Ibid., p. 194.
7. Ibid., p. 194.
8. Ibid., p. 194.
9. Garner, Gerald W., *Chief, The Reporters are Here*, Springfield, Thomas, 1987, p. 57.
10. Kelly, Patricia, *Police and the Media*, Bridging Troubled Waters, Springfield, Thomas, 1987, p. 71.
11. Ibid., p. 57.
12. Ibid., p. 145.
13. Ibid., p. 149.
14. Ibid., p. 67.
15. Rosendaum, Dennis P., Laurakus, Paul J., Lurgio, Arthur J., Crime Stoppers:

A National Evaluation, Washington, D.C., U.S. Department of Justice, National Institute of Justice, Research in Brief, September 1986.

16. Vaughn, Jerald R., Presentation in New Orleans, IACP, Drug Control Strategy Conference, April 1987, National League of Cities.

17. Gropper, Bernard G., Probing the Links Between Drugs and Crime, Washington, D.C., U.S. Department of Justice, National Institute of Justice, Research in Brief, 1985.

18. Learning to Say No, *Time*, September 15, 1988, p. 73.

19. Ibid.

20. Tom Adams, Director, Just Say No Program, *Time*, N.Y., September 15, 1988, p. 73.

21. Doren, Steve, VOCA is Doing the Job, N.Y., NOVA Newsletter, Volume 12, Number 6, June 1988.

22. Hassel, Conrad V., Law Enforcement and Behavioral Sciences: Closing the Gap, Washington, D.C., FBI Training Manual, 1986, p. 1.

23. Olin, Ronald W., Tactical Crisis Management, Washington, D.C., *FBI Law Enforcement Bulletin*, November 1980, p. 5.

24. Cohen, William A., and Nurit, *Top Executive Performance*, N.Y., Wiley and Sons, 1984, pp. 120–22.

25. Whitham, Donald C., *Management Reform and Police Executives*, Fairfax, 1986, The Bureaucrat, Institute for Public Management, George Mason University.

26. Cribbin, James J., Leadership, Your Competitive Edge, N.Y., American Management Associations, 1981, Amacom, All Rights Reserved. Reprinted by Permission of the Publisher.

27. Billy, C., Moving Up, PTST, PETG, or N.Y., p. 119.

28. Ibid., p. 135.

29. Slomas, Richard S., *No Nonsense Management*, N.Y., Macmillan, 1987, p. 67.

30. Hunsaker, Phillip L., Alessandra, Anthony J., *The Art of Managing People*, N.Y., Simon and Schuster, 1980, pp. 1–2.

31. Brown, Steve W., *13 Fatal Errors Managers Make*, N.Y., Berkeley, 1987, p. 62.

32. Crosby, Phillip B., *Running Things*, McGraw-Hill, N.Y., 1986, p. 227.

33. Tichy, Noel M., Davanna, Mary Ann, *The Transformational Leader*, N.Y., Wiley, 1986, p. 84.

34. Ibid., p. 84.

35. Ibid., p. 85.

36. Whitham, Donald C., *Management Reform and Police Executives*, Fairfax, 1986, The Bureaucrat, Institute for Public Management, George Mason University.

37. Schultz, Donald O., *Modern Police Administration*, Houston, Gulf Publishing, 1979, p. 52.

38. Executive Skills Enrichment—NIBM Seminars in Print, National Institute of Business Management, Inc., N.Y., 1985.

39. Ibid., Reprint of pp. 78–83 with Permission from NBIM, Inc.

40. Skolnick, Jerome H., Bayley, David H., Community of Policing: Issues and Practices Around the World, Washington, D.C., 1988, National Institute of Justice, p. 16.

41. Ibid., p. 17.
42. Ibid., p. 12.
43. Ibid., p. 12.
44. Ibid., p. 14.
45. Ibid., p. 16.
46. Ibid., p. 18.
47. Ibid., p. 72.
48. Ibid., p. 86.
49. Seelmeyer, John, A Citizen's Police Academy, *Law and Order,* December 1987.
50. Holden, Richard N., *Modern Police Management,* Englewood Cliffs, Prentice Hall, 1986, p. 12.
51. Elliot, J.F., *The New Police,* Springfield, Thomas, 1973, p. 8.
52. Ellis, Terrance L., Bailey, Ralph A., Healthy Police Officers Are Cost Effective Police Officers, League of California Cities, 1983, *Western City Magazine.*
53. Hamilton, Robert A., One State Fights Officer Stress, Hendon, October 1987, *Law and Order Magazine.*
54. Gortner, Harold F., *Administration in the Public Sector,* N.Y., Wiley, 1977, p. 315.
55. Swanson, Charles R., Territo, Leonard, *Police Administration: Structures, Processes, and Behavior,* N.Y., McMillan, 3rd, 1983, p. 345.
56. More, Harry W., Kenney, John P., *The Police Executive Handbook,* Springfield, Thomas, 1986, p. 159.
57. Eastham, George D., Eastham, Ester M., Municipal Police Administration, Washington, D.C., ICMA, 1971, p. 43.
58. Commission on Accreditation for Law Enforcement Agencies, Inc., Standards Manual, 1987, Reprinted with Permission.
59. Pearson, Jack, National Accreditation: A Valuable Management Tool, Los Angeles, *Western City Magazine,* League of California Cities, July 1983.
60. Heinly, David R., Keeping an Eye on Crime Trends, *Security World Magazine,* May 1986.
61. Ibid.
62. Ibid.
63. Ibid.
64. Ibid.

REFERENCES

Davis, James R., *Tactical Crisis Management,* El Cajon, California, Police Training Systems, 1987.
Smith, Eugene M., *Handbook for Hostage Negotiations,* N.Y. Harper and Row, 1980.
Goodman, Stanley J., *How to Manage a Turnaround,* N.Y., McMillan, 1982.
Garmire, Bernard L., Local Government Police Management, Washington, D.C., Institute of Training in Municipal Administration, ICMA, 1977.
U.S. Department of Justice, FBI, Uniform Crime Reporting Handbook, Washington, D.C., U.S. Government Printing Office, 1987.

Rosenbaum, Dennis P., Lurgio, Arthur J., Laurakus, Paul J., Crime Stoppers: A National Evaluation, Washington, D.C., U.S. Department of Justice, Research in Brief, September 1986.

Skolnick, Jerome H., Bayley, David H., Community Policing: Issues and Practices Around the World, Washington, D.C., 1988, National Institute of Justice.

Commission on Accreditation for Law Enforcement Agencies, Inc., The Standard Manual of Law Enforcement Agency Accreditation Program, May 1987.

Pearson, Jack, National Accreditation: A Valuable Management Tool, Los Angeles, *Western City Magazine,* League of California Cities, July 1983.

Chapter 5

ARCHITECTURAL ADJUSTMENTS

THE SINKING OF THE ISLAND MENTALITY

As newer models of police managers assume control of the reins of organizational direction, they will learn in their own way what others before them learned; new problems arise much more quickly than old ones are solved. The newer models do have an advantage. Their organizational climates are different, conducive to a lasting and meaningful alteration of police practices. Better personnel have been employed in the recent past and are better adapted to the purpose of this work. More self-criticism exists within police service. A premium is finally being put forth by many agencies to research, field test and, most importantly, include their officers who are doing the work in the decision-making processes which directly affect their performances. It has taken a generation of attitude and educational adjustment for these indicators of a system's change to come about in a recognizable format. Planners will recognize that in reality, the service has not been the catalyst for this evolution; society has. The organization has become more of a true reflection of society. The island mentality still exists and often absorbs the necessary change agents into the organization. Influences reverberate and lead to a deeper appreciation of the necessity of freshness for future eras of police managers, but it will take more time.

It is not unreasonable to anticipate that the 1990s will be the first decade since the 1960s in which police organizations will see themselves outwardly changing for the better. Scholars and practitioners may eventually look upon the 1990s the way the current planners view the 1960s. Communities will undoubtedly witness this outward change much quicker than they did in the 1960s. The increased understanding of police work and the enhanced participation in crime-solving problems will establish a never-before-experienced bond between citizens and police. The bond will add another dimension to the service, as well as a more pronounced visibility and a deeper appreciation of the complexities of police work which will, in turn, further cement this partnership.

VISION VS. REACTION

The ideal manager of the 1990s will combine cost-consciousness with creativity and a new ingredient: caring.[1] A more imaginative set of tactics erected under the principles of vision, not **reaction,** may surface as the norm, not the exception. This version of manager who replaces the single-tracked autocrat will not only communicate and stand for improvements in police service, but will be the major reason many future problems in law enforcement are resolved by frontline people who deal with the problems on a daily basis. The decisional paralysis, the denying that there is a crisis, and the delaying of major changes should cease, little by little.[2]

BREAKING WITH TRADITION

As planners undertake the tasks that lie ahead, they must develop an atmosphere that permeates the entire organization, but which is managed in such a way that it is not disorienting or threatening.[3] The substantive issues which face law enforcement must be in the forefront, and the planner must not allow preoccupation with mechanical improvements, as witnessed during past decades. The practitioner in the 1990s will be the architect designing the future framework of police service. More road maps will be needed, and more issues will need to be discussed in exchanges between administrators from all over the country from every size police agency in the United States.

Seeing to it that freshman supervisors are exposed to quality training, focusing on development of their talents towards becoming effective engineers who enhance the human relations side of management, is a requisite. Breaking with tradition and calling upon private industry and external associations to instruct special seminars which tackle management and supervision problems will incorporate the proper blend of leadership into the workings of police organizations in the 1990s. Improved and updated books and writings for police service libraries will provide managers at all levels the resources through which to seek new avenues in problem-solving, and will further compliment the development of leadership skills.

It is important that people in all organizations believe their work is important to the organization and that their organization cares for them as individuals.[4] Police officers usually agree and feel that their work is truly important; after all, they are always the first to see the reasons and purposes requiring laws and the consequences of a society with order. But the service has done little to make officers believe that their organizations care for them, an area in which vast improvements can be made by the manager of the 1990s.

Unjustified fears of **nationalization** should be discounted. While there are trends to nationalize standards under which police service should operate, little evidence exists which supports a contention that a nationalized police corp would even be possible under our existing form of government. Community policing trends forcefully offset any perceived catalyst which might be viewed as a threat to America's decentralized law enforcement practices. Perhaps the fear of nontraditional influences on police organizations seeds these types of concerns when, all the while, those seeds only continue to widen the crack in the isolation practices which were so painfully revealed in the 1960s.

CHALLENGES UNREALATED TO CRIME

Many police agents are maturing at a fast pace. The advancements are far from uniform for all police departments, but the current thrust should serve as motivation to keep up with the advancements in this field (even if the field cannot keep up with the pace of advancements in other dynamic organizations in society). However, planners who research and study only those advancements in the police field will fail in the 1990s. A certain tempo has been established in police service, one that has been conspicuously absent in previous eras. The true challenge is found in whether or not the tempo will be picked up throughout the service, not just by a few organizations. For the first time in American history, the police service is faced with problems and challenges that are not solely related to crime. A broader approach is now required, one that is somewhat unrelated to technological solutions.[5]

ENDNOTES

1. McCormick, John, Powell, Bill, Management for the 1990s, N.Y., *Newsweek*, April 25, 1988.

2. Levine, Charles H., Strategic Management, Washington, D.C., Law and Public Affairs, Public Administration Review, ASPA, 1985.
3. Goldstein, Herman, *Policing a Free Society,* Cambridge, Ballinger, 1977, p. 309.
4. Whitham, Donald C., Mitchell, David T., Higher Performance Through Organizational Development, Washington, D.C., *FBI Law Enforcement Bulletin,* February, 1985.
5. Eastham, George D., Eastham, Ester M., Municipal Police Administration, ICMA, Washington, D.C., 1969, p. 219.

REFERENCES

Goldstein, Herman, *Policing a Free Society,* Cambridge, Ballinger, 1977.

Chapter 6

A DISTINCTIVE LEADERSHIP,
A DISTINCTIVE PROFESSION

Since 1929, more than 30 **studies** of police service have received national attention. The watershed Wickersham Report is widely recognized as one of the first to bring to light the woeful inadequacies of law enforcement and its management. To read one of these reports is to read them all; the problems seldom change, and never disappear. The only significant difference is in the updating of terminology.[1] Most of these visions, however, are merely lists of things that are wrong with police service; seldom do they offer practical suggestions on making the corrections.[2] Flooding the service with federal funding, once considered a solution, briefly submerged criminal justice in oceans of fiscal soundness and resulted in technological and educational advancement. But, while that advancement stabilized law enforcement, it did not immediately cure the ills of poorly managed organizations; they needed more than a new suit of clothes.

The practitioner's **road map** in this text has outlined more than 20 areas which offer practice alternatives to the problems facing the service today and through the next decade. Future studies of police service are apt to concentrate on three general areas: leadership development, professionalism, and general management.

LEADERSHIP DEVELOPMENT

There is no need to dig deeply for an explanation of our failure to develop a reservoir of competent leadership in the police field. This country has tenaciously clung to the concept that leadership of a police agency should be drawn not only from within the police field, but from within the agency. Yet no provisions have been made to assure that police agencies systematically produce people with requisite qualifications for leadership. Worse still, the citizenry and the police together have stubbornly adhered to provisions governing recruitment and promotion of police personnel that appear to have the opposite effect... indeed if one sets out to design a system to prevent and discourage the police from developing their own leadership capabilities, it would be difficult to come up with a more sure-fire scheme than that which currently exists. . . .

Herman Goldstein, Policing a Free Society

In an attempt to institute **fairness** as well as to meet standards handed down by courts across the country, police agencies have selected their leaders and future managers on the basis of written tests or successful completion of an assessment center. The concept is sound but the results too often cosmetic. Most frequently, specialized book knowledge people wind up running police organizations, showing little ability to implement their knowledge in a practical situation.[3] The theory here is that the best will finish at the top, but a few specialized book knowledge people will always advance into the leadership ranks. That may be acceptable to most governing bodies, since these concepts do reduce litigations and meet the general test of fairness. However, by embracing this concept, police agencies must live with one of two choices. Their first choice is to struggle on with the book knowledge leader, the one most often found to have few management skills, a mundane past performance record, and little, if any, social awareness . . . in short, marginal abilities to lead. Their second choice is to be content with the **fairness** of this concept for leadership selection, accept the fact that **book knowledge** managers will win advancement, and to spend time and money on training those people through programs designed to bring this borderline leader up to par. If they become more successful in their leadership talents, they should be given more and more responsibility; if they cannot, they should not be allowed to manage.

Most of this situation can be linked to civil service. O. W. Wilson's unconventional wisdom made him a staunch opponent of some civil service standards imposed on police organizations. Wilson contended that promotional systems based upon this doctrine hampered police chiefs in selecting the most qualified personnel for promotion and leadership positions.[4] He also opposed civil service restrictions which prevented police service from considering leadership potential at the hiring level.

Civil service has its benefits for government and society. The protection afforded employees has been a necessary principle, but civil service is often seen as only **requiring mediocrity**; once the position is acquired, minimal effort is necessary to keep it. Nowhere can the harmful effects of civil service be seen so dramatically as in police organization management. Civil service is the primary demon that prevents current and serious consideration to the concept of lateral entry for police managers. Unless more training is afforded to the marginal, **book knowledge promotee,** or until a lateral entry pool becomes a reality, police administrators are likely to be stuck with a haphazard managerial balancing act.

These problems are related by three long-standing concepts: (1) Only law enforcement personnel understand this problem; (2) duties of law enforcement agencies should be subject to local control; and (3) lack of understanding by both government officials and the public as to the complexity and importance of the law enforcement management function. Because of this lack of knowledge, police managers have been trained as **political bums** in many areas.[5] This is most frequently seen in the small police agencies.

Planners must educate government officials and the public as to the need of progressive police leadership. The problem needs to be understood by more than those who live it. Local government and community control certainly works to the advantage of most police departments; this local control may also be the avenue through which lateral entry could be established. There is little, if anything, that prevents a city from establishing its own lateral entry policy to enhance all levels of police leadership, not just the chief's position.

TAKING A STAND ON MANAGEMENT PRACTICES

Planners in the future will be more apt to appreciate and understand the single assumption upon which all theories of management rest—"that good management can be taught, learned, and applied."[6] More has to be done than has in the past. New supervisors cannot be turned loose in expectations that they will automatically and efficiently handle all the problems they will encounter. Planners will have to take a firm stand and protect their organization from those who are not willing to learn. They will have to accept the fact that many people cannot be managers; they lack the foundation from which good management is derived. This does not mean that they were born weak; they simply lack the foundation to prepare them for administration.[7]

One of the many reasons poor managers cannot learn to be good managers is their unwillingness to acknowledge that they need to learn anything about management. This reason is not foreign to police service; many of today's administrators came from the school of thought which suggested that in order to become a leader, you must only be appointed to a **position** or be given a title. Good managers are willing to learn and, most importantly, are comfortable with change. As pointed out earlier in this text, poor managers will quickly discard anything that is not in conformity to their preconceived notions.[8] An interesting point made by Richard Holden in his **Modern Police Management** text is that managerial capacities seem to be strongly related to character flaws of the manager. Those who lack integrity, hard-core autocrats, know-it-alls, those unable to make decisions, the Peter Principled individuals who are in over their heads, the knit-pickers, those who waste time on minor details, and those who politic to prevent responsibility from falling on their shoulders all suffer from their inability to form the proper chemistry between them and their subordinates; they fail to elicit respect. It's a simple premise: good managers work well with people; poor managers do not.[9]

In order for police service to advance beyond the disjointed, multiple standards of management under which they have operated for years, planners must pull together and view police service as a whole. Managerial upgrades, based on widely accepted and proven administrative techniques, must be adopted. When the majority, instead of the minority, of police planners begin similar, up-to-date and effective management practices, the core of police service throughout the country will change for the better. The key to this approach is getting practitioners to think alike without regarding the necessary **community ingredients** which make departments a reflection of their respective communities.

THE CALLS FOR PROFESSIONALISM

In order to understand exactly what **professionalism** means to current day police officers, planners should ask not only the next recruit class about their views on professionalism, but poll some veteran officers and managers. Planners may find that they will receive as many different responses as they would if they asked a room full of attorneys to interpret the same Supreme Court decision. **Professionalism** for today's police officer means a lot of different things. This is one reason why true professionalism is still a mantle yet to be awarded in any serious degree to police service. The calls for professionalism have in many cases been based on misinterpretation, misapplication, misrepresentation, and miscalculation.[10]

Those who insist that police service has already attained professionalism fail to recognize that professional status is not the same for all occupational groups. Police officers may often find that they pursued a **professional status** primarily in the hope of obtaining its perceived rewards.[11] The social role of police vastly differs from the social role of other recognized professions. Societal delegation and discretionary powers are the factors upon which police most often claim are the centerpieces of their **profession.** The more traditionally acclaimed professions, physicians and lawyers, base their claim on personal expertise. The police must deal with anyone and everyone who calls upon them for service; recognized professionals do not. Professional status, in its most acceptable and recognizable form, only comes about when the public accepts that professionals know more about what is good for their clients than the clients themselves.[12] Obviously, this is not yet true with police service. External influences, even when necessary, most often disclose that many politicians and legislative groups direct police organizations as though they truly do know more than the practitioners. In some cases they may, but the point is not lessened by the practice in those cases.

Planners need a different view of professionalism, one that can be filtered through the ranks of the service. Rather than seeing professionalism as a point to be reached, too many still see the professional status as a reward along with the rewards that go to other recognized professionals. This would mean that in comparison, police deserve better wages, greater social stature, greater public respect and deference, and, above all, organizational autonomy.[13] Higher wages and greater social status for police officers is fully justified without regards to the issues of professionalism, so thinking that **professionalism** will automatically be awarded once higher pay and greater social status is achieved is sloppy thinking. Efforts to upgrade must and will continue, but planners need to think beyond terminology and build police service into a profession that is not in superficial competition with other recognized professional occupations.

A FINAL NOTE ON LEADERSHIP

Leadership is one of the most observed but least understood phenomena in the world.[14] According to Burt Nanus and Warren Bennis, authors of Leaders: Strategies for Taking Control, the distinguishing talent possessed by leaders who can make a difference is their ability to envision.[15] They go on to state that these types of leaders are capable of seeing the entire organization, the complex environment, and the interaction of the two as a single entity. Further, they are able to project this view into the future and describe a favorable future for the organization. They articulate this vision to others and provide them with a sense of meaning, thus inspiring trust in others—partly because of their steadfastness to their vision.[16] This definition of leader stresses and addresses the morality and integrity of leaders, thus ensuring the trust of their subordinates.

Planners in the 1990s must become the type of leaders described by Nanus and Bennis. When they are in doubt, they will have to research, explore, read, and take some risks. A critical ingredient to the future success of police organizations will be found in their leadership. Although police leaders cannot single-handedly upgrade police service, there is no other single group as important to this process.[17]

ENDNOTES

1. Elliott, J.F., *The New Police,* Springfield, Thomas, 1973, p. 3.
2. Ibid., p. 69.
3. Ibid., p. 63.
4. Thibault, Edward A., Lynch, Lawrence M., McBride, R. Bruce, Englewood Cliffs, Prentice Hall, 1985, p. 49.
5. Holden, Richard N., Englewood Cliffs, Prentice Hall, 1986, p. 14.
6. Ibid., p. 9.
7. Ibid., p. 9.
8. Ibid., p. 10.
9. Ibid., p. 11.
10. Potts, Lee W., *Responsible Police Administration,* University, University of Alabama Press, 1983, p. 144.
11. Ibid., p. 145.
12. Ibid., p. 148.
13. Ibid., p. 155.
14. Burns, James McGregor, Leadership, New York, Harper and Row, 1978, p. 9.
15. Bennis, Warren, Nanus, Burt, *Leadership: Strategies for Taking Control,* New York, Harper and Row, 1985, pp. 216–219.
16. Whitham, Donald C., Transformational Police Leadership, Washington, D.C., *FBI Law Enforcement Bulletin,* December 1987.
17. Ibid.

REFERENCES

Elliott, J.F., *The New Police,* Springfield, Thomas, 1973.

Goldstein, Herman, *Policing a Free Society,* Cambridge, Ballinger, 1977.

Potts, Lee W., *Responsible Police Administration,* University, University of Alabama Press, 1983.

Whitham, Donald C., Transformational Police Leadership, Washington, D.C., *FBI Law Enforcement Bulletin,* December 1987.

AFTERWORD

By definition, the decision-making process is based on value systems. Most decisions are made subjectively, whether or not managers want to admit it. The values of police managers who will lead throughout the 1990s will set the future course for police service, just as values of managers have in the past. But this era is more likely to steer away from low-yield strategies and reflect the overall changes in attitudes and values which are mirrored throughout society.

This book will find a ready audience; but, while the road map may not be for every police manager or every police agency, the cardinal points and concepts underscored here are:

- Change is the only true constant. . . .
- Know where your organization has been in order to understand how it is to move from where it is into the future. . . .
- Do not get so involved in techniques that people, especially the ones who perform the work, are forgotten. . . .
- An organization will not be effective when errors or mistakes are repeated. . . .
- Police service cannot advance itself if it is isolated from other dynamic organizations in society. . . .
- Managers must have an agenda. . . .
- Police organizations are unlikely to be better than their leaders. . . .

INDEX

Feilding, Henry, 4
Fiscal (*see also* Police service, Cost,
    Compensation)
    budgetary processes, 119–118
    external funding, 121–122
    fundamental planning, 120–121
Florida State Police, 70
Forecasts (*see also* Police service)
    future of law enforcement issues, 28–32
Future (*see also* Forecasts)
    a look into, 23
    predictions, 25–32

G

General Health Corporation, 118
Georgia State Police, 70
Goldstein, Herman, 140

H

Habit, 11
Health (*see also* Police service)
    concerns for future of, 118
    costs of career survival, 117
    mandatory programs, 118
    officer's concerns on, 117–119
History
    perspectives, 4
    media and police, 45–46
Holden, Richard, 142
Hoover, J. Edgar, 24
Hostage Negotiation (*see also* Tactical
    incident management)
    evolution and need for, 81–82
    considerations of forecasts, 83
    merging of efforts, 83
    SWAT and public criticism, 81

I

International Associations of Chiefs of
    Police, 23, 96, 123
International City Managers Association, 96
Institute of Police Management and
    Technology (*see also* Drug
    enforcement)
    training by, 71
Inflation, 8

Interactive management, 36–37
Interagency politics (*see also* Politics)
    basic strategies of, 103
    chronic games of, 103–105
    curbing, 105–106
    destructive, 105
    harmful effects of, 102
    written and oral, 103–104
Isolation of police organizations, 9

J

Johnson, President Lyndon, 6

K

Kelly, Clarence, M. 36
Kenney, John, 120

L

Law Enforcement (*see also* Police service)
    as big business, 18
Lateral entry, 17, 36
Leadership (*see also* Management)
    academic theories of, 16
    change of styles for, 30
    compensation and, 99, 101
    definition, 16
    development of, 139–140
    ethics of, 88–89
    formal power of, 16
    informal power of, 17
    interactive, 36–37
    political appointments and, 96–97
    political responsibilities and, 95
    redefining, 35
    understanding of, 143–144
Lexington, Kentucky Police, 58, 67, 78
London Metropolitan Police, 45
Los Angeles Police, 25, 77, 102

M

Management (*see also* Leadership)
    attitudes of poor, 142
    blending of, 86
    costs for, 3
    crisis, 13